MY SOUL IS IN HAITI

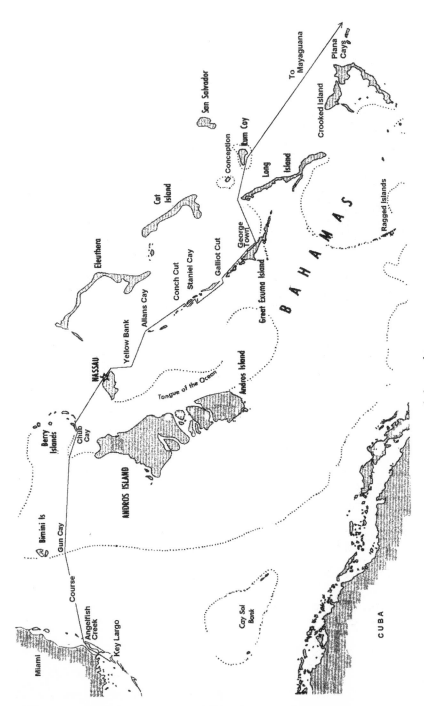

The Bahamas. Courtesy of Kiran Jayaram, http:/jarogers.com/bahamap.htm.

My Soul Is in Haiti

Protestantism in the Haitian Diaspora of the Bahamas

Bertin M. Louis, Jr.

NEW YORK UNIVERSITY PRESS
New York and London

NEW YORK UNIVERSITY PRESS
New York and London
www.nyupress.org

References to Internet websites (URLs) were accurate at the time of writing. Neither the author nor New York University Press is responsible for URLs that may have expired or changed since the manuscript was prepared.

Library of Congress Cataloging-in-Publication Data
Louis, Bertin M., Jr.
My soul is in Haiti : Protestantism in the Haitian diaspora of the Bahamas / Bertin Louis.
pages cm   Includes bibliographical references and index.
ISBN 978-1-4798-0993-6 (hardback)
1. Protestantism—Haiti. 2. Haitians—Bahamas. 3. Identification (Religion)—Political aspects—Haiti. I. Title.
BX4835.H2L68   2014
280'.4089969729407296—dc23   2014025209

New York University Press books are printed on acid-free paper, and their binding materials are chosen for strength and durability. We strive to use environmentally responsible suppliers and materials to the greatest extent possible in publishing our books.

Manufactured in the United States of America

10 9 8 7 6 5 4 3 2 1

Also available as an ebook

To my grandmother, Alice Jean-Louis Fougy, founder of La Grande Cohorte,
and my mother, Gerda F. Louis. Toujours Joyeux.

Soldats de Christ et Haïtiens,	Soldiers of Christ and Haitians,
Du ciel nous sommes citoyens,	We are citizens of heaven,
Dans la Parole du Seigneur,	In the Word of God,
Nous trouvons le seul vrai bonheur.	We've found the only true happiness.
Refrain:	*Refrain:*
Sauve, Seigneur, bénis,	Save, O Lord, Bless,
Notre chère Haïti!	Our dear Haiti!
Petite nation,	Small nation,
Avance vers Sion,	Go forward to Zion,
À Dieu consacre-toi,	Consecrate yourself to God,
Fais de Jésus ton Roi.	Let Jesus be your King (your ruler).
Sauve, Seigneur,	Save, O Lord,
Bénis notre chère Haïti!	Bless our dear Haiti!
Soldats de Christ et Haïtiens,	Soldiers of Christ and Haitians,
Soyons unis à tous les siens,	Every one of us united,
Car dans le Testament Nouveau,	For in the New Testament,
Il nous a marqués de son sceau.	It has marked us with its stamp.
Compatriotes Haïtiens,	Haitian Compatriots,
Du ciel devenez citoyens,	Become a citizen of heaven,
Chantez avec nous désormais:	Sing with us from now on:
Haïti pour Christ à jamais!	Haiti for Christ forever!

—French hymn number 320 in the "Chants Nationaux Chrétiens" (National Christian Songs) section of *Chants D'espérance* (Songs of Hope)

CONTENTS

ACKNOWLEDGMENTS

Many people are responsible for the formation and completion of this book and I would like to thank all of them.

This book would not have been possible without the support of the following pastors: Chérélus Exanté of New Haitian Mission Baptist Church, Kevin Pierre of International Tabernacle of Praise Ministries, Inc., and Dieunous Senatus and Antoine Saint Louis of Victory Chapel Church of the Nazarene in New Providence, Bahamas. I also thank my Haitian research participants, who allowed me to enter their homes and divulged their thoughts and beliefs to me. Many of them risked their lives getting to the Bahamas and continue to live a tenuous life there. I truly appreciate their willingness to talk to me in the face of their daily struggles. I also thank my Bahamian participants of Haitian descent who continue to struggle for full inclusion in Bahamian society. I realize that it was difficult for them to recount the painful memories that render them stateless and without dignity in the Bahamas. I thank them for their participation and admire their resilience in the face of adversity. My hope is that this book challenges the stereotypical views of Haitians in the Bahamas and contributes to a discussion about how Haitians and Bahamians can live together with respect for each other and build a better Bahamas together.

I also would like to thank my colleagues and friends in the Bahamas who helped me understand the structural issues of the Bahamas that troubled me during my sojourn. Their kindness and generosity allowed me to balance my view of Nassau (New Providence) and of the Bahamas overall. In particular, I thank the late Thaddeus MacDonald, Ian

Strachan, Virginia Ballance, Mtumwa Kmt, William Fielding, Novado, the Hanna Family of Capt's Place on St. Albans Drive, and Mary Ann Higgs. I also thank Katherine Stewart-Gibson and Lisa Moxey of the American Embassy who facilitated a smooth entry into New Providence for me.

When I began studying Haitian Protestantism in the United States in 2000, the main person who described this growing religious movement to me was Jean L. Paillan (Pastor Lesly), former head pastor of Truth and Grace Haitian Christian Church in Saint Peters, Missouri. I am eternally grateful for his help throughout this process and his insightful comments that have helped me see Haitian Protestantism in a new light.

During my visit to Haiti in 2002, I was able to navigate Port-au-Prince with the help of my maternal aunt, Maude Jacob, and her husband, Joseph Pierre Jacob, and my cousins, Deborah Jacob Villefranche and Keitel Jacob. I also thank my late cousin, Georges Jean-Louis, for guiding me through the streets of Port-au-Prince and my Haitian Creole tutor, Louinès Volny, who introduced me to the current Haitian Creole orthographic system. Volny also worked with me on my pronunciation, writing, and reading skills. Pastor Soliny Védrine helped me throughout this process and I am grateful and indebted to him for his help in making this book a reality (*Jezu se sovè mwen, men Pastè Solini se paspò mwen!*). I also thank my other maternal aunts, Gladys Louissaint, Ghislaine Fougy, and Emmeline Védrine, and my maternal uncle, Fritz Fougy, for their prayers and support from my birth to this current accomplishment. None of this could have been completed without their help, ideas, comments, and beliefs. I also thank my maternal grandparents, the late Alice Jean-Louis Fougy (Manman Alice), founder of La Grande Cohorte, and the late Jonas Fougy (Papa Jonas), who laid the foundation of Protestantism in my family.

I thank John Bowen, for his constructive criticism throughout the process and for helping me become a cultural anthropologist. I also thank Wayne Fields, Rebecca Lester, Shanti Parikh, Joseph Thompson, and James Wertsch for their comments on my research. Wayne, in particular, allowed me to put my trip to the Bahamas in perspective and I am indebted to his support and timely words of encouragement. I thank the members of the Washington University Anthropology writing group, with special thanks to Laura Cochrane and Vanessa Hildebrand. I also thank the Washington University Program in International and Area Studies, the Fulbright program, and the Lambda Alpha Anthropology National Honors Society for the financial support that helped me conduct research in the United States, Haiti, and the Bahamas.

I thank the anonymous reviewers for their critical comments that have strengthened this book. I am indebted to Erik Schiller, who helped me through various stages of this project. Thank you very much to Cawist François and Devin Towles for their transcription services and and to Julia Thomas, Ermitte St. Jacques, Todne Thomas, Aimee Villarreal, and Celucien L. Joseph for their help. I also would like to thank Jennifer Hammer, my editor at New York University Press, who believed in my work, provided sage input, and waited patiently for the completion of this text. I must also thank my colleagues at the University of Tennessee: Rosalind Hackett, for introducing me to Jennifer, Rebecca Klenk and Karl Jost for their help during the early stages of this project, and Andy Kramer, for facilitating the time and space to complete this project.

I thank my church family at Saint Paul A.M.E. Zion Church of Maryville, Tennessee, with special thanks to Willa Estell for her spiritual guidance and prayers. I also thank Jama Woods, who helped my family with the care of my children while I wrote this book. I cannot forget Sharon Hannum who has helped my family with emotional and spiritual support. Thank you also for helping me with the title of this book.

I am grateful for the support of the Henderson family with special thanks to Janis and Clyde Henderson for their continuous support. I also thank my daughters, Nia Janis Henderson-Louis and Jocelyn Gerda Henderson-Louis, for their support and for accepting the numerous times that I was physically absent while working on this book. This text is yours as well.

I am also most grateful to my wife, Frances Henderson, whose encouragement edifies me and reminds me of who I am on those occasions when I forget. I would not have been able to finish this book without your support of my work and my being. Thank you for juggling your schedule to care for our children and facilitating time and space for me to complete this project. Your support sustains me and your intellect continues to challenge me. You have helped me become a better scholar, a better man, and, most importantly, a better human being.

I thank my brother, Gardy Louis, for all of his support over the years and my sister, Benjie Louis, whose prayers, support, and invaluable editing and proofreading skills were indispensable and central to the creation and completion of this text.

Finally, I must acknowledge the gifts I received from my parents that made this book possible. I owe my desire to lead a "life of the mind" and my interest in so many things Haitian to my father, Bertin Louis, Sr. I inherited my interest in Haitian Protestantism primarily from my mother, Gerda Fougy Louis, who kept the religious traditions of her family alive in ours. This book is for both of them. Hopefully, Haitians and other humans across the globe will one day be able to lead dignified lives, as was the hope of our ancestors centuries ago during the Haitian Revolution.

PRONUNCIATION OF HAITIAN CREOLE TERMINOLOGY

Throughout the book, I use the current Haitian orthographic system that symbolizes the spoken language of Haitian Creole. Established in Haiti in the 1980s, each symbol in the current Haitian Creole orthographic system represents only one sound. Consonants are sounded as they are in English, every vowel is pronounced separately and all the letters are pronounced in a word. For example, activity in English is "ak-tee-vee-tay" (*aktivite*) in Haitian Creole. The following list summarizes the pronunciation of vowels in Haitian Creole:

a is sounded like "o" in pot
e is sounded like "ay" in day
è is sounded like "e" in get
i is sounded like "ee" in greed
o is sounded like "oo" in book
ò is sounded like "o" in born
ou is sounded like "o" in move

There are nasalized sounds in Haitian Creole, as well, like *an* in *mouvman* (movement), *en* in *genyen* (to win, to beat), and *on* like *milyon* (million). An additional sound in Haitian Creole, *en*, is not found in English. *En* is nasalized and is similar to the *en* sound in the word *envy*. You find an example of that sound in the word *gouvenen* (to govern, to direct). *Ch* in Haitian Creole is pronounced like words beginning in *sh* in English like *shower*. An example of a *ch* word is *chita* (sit).

Introduction

Brother Magloire of Victory Chapel Church of the Nazarene was explaining to me the difference between Protestants and Christians among Haitian migrants in the Bahamas.[1] He noted that you had to observe how someone functioned in society: Does the person serve God and manifest a devout *karacktè* (character), or does he or she engage in acts considered to be sinful, such as attending dance parties, smoking, or wearing make-up? His observations highlight a curious finding I stumbled upon while conducting fieldwork about Haitian Protestant religious practice among migrants in the Bahamas. Some migrants regard Protestant and Christian as two very different identities, though anthropologists and religious studies scholars consider both terms as similar. In Haitian religious life, *Protestant* describes a religious movement that began in Haiti in the nineteenth century. The term is generally used in Haiti and the Haitian diaspora to refer to a person who practices some form of Protestant Christianity, such as the Adventist, Baptist, and Methodist faiths and Pentecostalism.[2] *Protestant* is also a pejorative term that is used privately among devout Haitian Protestants to describe other migrants in their diasporic religious community who engage in sinful behavior. Devout Haitian Protestant migrants in the Bahamas consider themselves as *Kretyen* (Christian) rather than *Pwotestan* (Protestant). They build their identities as *Kretyen* around (1) their adherence to shared, cultural norms of Protestant Christianity from their native Haiti regarding their appearance and comportment, and (2) their *krent pou Bondyè* (fear of God) which is reflected in proper appearance and comportment.

What is significant about this conceptualization of *Kretyen* versus *Pwotestan* is that it reveals a deeper dynamic in the lives of Protestant migrants from Haiti to the Bahamas—a receiving country in which approximately one in five people are now Haitian born or Haitian descended. Their ideas about religion illuminate how they think about their identities in a society that is hostile toward them. Their thinking also reveals how their religious beliefs help these devout human beings deal with exploitation and marginalization in the Bahamas and to advance a political and moral agenda for their Haitian homeland. At the heart of devout Haitian Protestant migrant life is a belief that religious authenticity is the key to both achieving their individual aspirations and transforming Haiti from the poorest country in the Western hemisphere into a viable, modern nation-state. By attending to the distinction between *Kretyen* and *Pwotestan* this book helps to explain why the typical Haitian migrant in the Bahamas now practices Protestant forms of Christianity.

Anthropologist Webb Keane (2007, 48) writes in his ethnography about Dutch Calvinist missionaries and their converts in Indonesia that the idea of modernity includes two distinctive features: rupture from a traditional past and progress into a better future. Modernity in the Caribbean required the twin barbarisms of the near-extermination of the indigenous peoples of the Caribbean and the kidnapping and enslavement of millions from sub-Saharan Africa.[3] In the case of what later came to be known as Haiti, the traditional past includes the 1697 Treaty of Ryswick between France and Spain, which established the French colony of Saint-Domingue. It used to be known as the "Pearl of the Antilles" because the industrialization of sugar in the region enriched its French absentee owners and transformed Saint-Domingue into one of the richest sugar colonies in history. The arduous labor required for sugar production resulted in the virtual eradication of the indigenous Taíno population and an average life span of only seven years for those Africans who survived the high mortality rates that stemmed from the forced marches from the interiors of Africa, the horrors of the Middle Passage, and the deadly seasoning process.[4]

Haiti's past also witnessed a struggle against chattel slavery. This struggle led to the destruction of plantation capitalism on the island of Hispaniola, which included the territories of present-day Haiti and the Dominican Republic. In what is known as the only successful slave revolt in human history, black people defeated the British and Spanish forces and achieved independence from their French colonial master to form the world's first black republic and extend the rights to liberty, equality, and fraternity to all Haitian citizens. In addition to its colonial roots and emancipatory struggle, Haiti's past also encapsulates a religious component that has contributed to the nation's bifurcated identity as a beacon of hope for some and a troubled nation for most.

Since Haiti's revolutionary beginnings, most Haitians have practiced Catholicism, the majority religion of Haiti, and Vodou. Vodou—a syncretic religion that incorporates Central and West African, European, and Amerindian beliefs—developed in Saint-Domingue and emerged from the context of chattel slavery and plantation culture. The practice of Vodou by enslaved Africans was an important factor that aided in their struggle for self-determination. As anthropologist Leslie Desmangles (1992, 6) has written, Haiti could not have become an independent nation without Vodou; its rituals provided the spirit of kinship that fueled the slaves' revolts against their colonial masters. Today, however, many Haitians are renouncing this past as a way to progress into a better future for themselves and their Haitian homeland. The embrace of a religious path that promises to lead to a better life in Haiti is part of a growing trend that is transforming the religious landscape of the region from the practice of Catholicism and Vodou (and other African-based religions) to the practice of Protestant forms of Christianity. Scholars have been somewhat slow to attend to this transformation; much of the research on Haiti and the Haitian diaspora still is focused on the two former religious traditions despite the fact that a large percentage of Haitians (and other formerly Catholic populations in Latin America) are now Protestant.

The practice of Protestant forms of Christianity up until recently has represented only a small fraction of Haiti's overall religious population.

However, as other parts of Catholic Latin America have turned Protestant, the growth and success of Protestantism has extended to Haiti. In 1930, for example, only 1.5 percent of the population of Haiti practiced Protestant forms of Christianity. Between 1930 and 1940, the population of Protestants tripled and between 1940 and 1950 it doubled. By 1977, 20 percent of the country had converted to Protestantism (Romain 2004, 429). It is currently estimated that about one third of Haiti is Protestant (Louis 2007, 194).[5]

The practice of Protestant forms of Christianity among Haitians in its diaspora throughout the United States is also rising, and Haitian Protestants have begun to outnumber Haitian Catholics in some US locales (Richman 2005). In New York City, Haitian Protestant churches—which were estimated to number more than one hundred in 2006— outnumber Haitian Catholic churches (see Ng 2006), suggesting that the number of Haitians who attend Protestant churches is rising and that Haitian Protestants may be a new religious majority among Haitians in the New York City area. This trend may be repeating itself in the American locales in which we find significant Haitian populations, such as Boston, Massachusetts, and Philadelphia, Pennsylvania.[6]

The Haitian practice of Protestant forms of Christianity among migrants in the Caribbean is also on the rise (Brodwin 2003a; 2003b).[7] When responding to a 2005 survey concerning the religion they practiced, 27.7 percent of Haitians interviewed in the Bahamas replied Catholic, whereas 29.1 percent claimed Anglican, Baptist, or Pentecostal (College of the Bahamas 2005, 100). These figures suggest that there is a new religious plurality among Haitians in the Bahamas, whereas in 1979, geographer Dawn Marshall (1979, xiii) remarked that the typical Haitian migrant was "almost certainly a Roman Catholic."

This book argues that Haitian Protestant migrants in the Bahamas reflect the growing trend toward Protestantism. For these migrants, a *Kretyen*, a devout Protestant, serves as a critique of their diasporic compatriots and also showcases their hopes of a future reshaping of Haiti into a Protestant Christian nation. Based on baptism by immersion in water and a life based on the culture and religious principles of Protestant Christianity in Haiti, most of my *Kretyen* research consultants believed that their personal salvation was guaranteed. The identity of *Kretyen* helped them both to critique what they considered to be wrong in the broader Haitian Protestant community of the Bahamas and to represent the type of citizen they believed Haiti needed in order to rectify its myriad social and economic ills.

The *Kretyen/Pwotestan* distinction is the result of two important and interrelated factors. The first is the growing practice of Protestant culture in Haiti and how Haitian Protestant migrants in the Bahamas use it to make meaning out of their daily experiences. Reverend Pat Robertson's comments after the Haitian earthquake in 2010 resonate with a similar Haitian Protestant worldview expressed to me during fieldwork in 2005. On January 12, 2010, a 7.0 earthquake devastated large parts of Port-au-Prince, Léogâne, and cities and towns along Haiti's Southern Peninsula. The earthquake destroyed much of the fragile urban infrastructure, claimed the lives of over two hundred thousand Haitians, and left over one million homeless. The day after this catastrophe, Robertson remarked on the 700 Club—a syndicated news show for the Christian Broadcasting Network that reaches over one billion households worldwide[8]—that centuries ago enslaved Africans toiling on the plantations of Saint-Domingue swore a "pact to the Devil" in order to gain their freedom from chattel slavery under the French.[9] The event, which Robertson analyzed through the lens of American Evangelical Christianity, was a Vodou ceremony known in the Haitian national narrative as *Bwa Kayiman* (Bois Caïman) that launched the Haitian Revolution (1791–1803). It was this supposed "pact with the Devil" that, according to Robertson, laid the foundations for the tragedy of the earthquake.

Robertson's remarks in the midst of this unimaginable tragedy sparked outrage and dismay, including condemnations (see Miller 2010) and essays (see Gates 2010) that critiqued his theological interpretation of Haitian history. Reverend Robertson's comments did not surprise me, however; my Haitian Protestant research consultants in New Providence,

Bahamas, had made similar comments five years earlier about the troubles of Haiti stemming from this pivotal Vodou ceremony, and some offered similar sentiments in the wake of the earthquake. At first glance, people familiar with Haitian history could view these comments by Haitian Protestant migrants as a form of self-hate. But this oppositional worldview stems, partly, from a Haitian Protestant rejection of the secular world. By viewing *Bwa Kayiman* as a moment when Haiti was "consecrated to the Devil," these devout migrants share a similar worldview to that of Reverend Robertson. They embrace a key component of a larger Haitian Protestant culture that rejects its Africanized roots in order to refashion Haitians into evangelical Christians and reintegrate Haiti as a respected nation into a larger global system that currently ruthlessly exploits them.

Although a number of Haitian Protestant denominations—including Adventists, Baptists, Methodists, Nazarenes, and Pentecostals—experience interdenominational tensions due to theological differences, they all share commonalities that make their practice of Protestantism distinct from the practice of Catholicism, the traditional majority religion of Haiti. One of these characteristics is a complete rejection of Vodou. Haitian Protestants, regardless of denominational affiliation, see Vodou as a backward way of life that keeps Haiti mired in endemic poverty and governmental corruption, and, in some cases, "curses" Haiti with ecological disasters like the 2010 earthquake.

The second factor that influences the use of the *Kretyen/Pwotestan* distinction is the normative exploitation of Haitians in the Bahamas. Their oppression is facilitated by the Bahamian state, codified in Bahamian law, and reflected in the organization of Bahamian society. As a result, Haitian migrants and Bahamians of Haitian descent, who are referred to as Haitian and Haitian-Bahamian, have become part of an underclass that continues to grow due to Haitian immigration and Bahamian laws that restrict social and economic opportunities to only those who can be defined as "Bahamian"—primarily black people with certain surnames, such as Bodie, Knowles, Moxey, Roker, Rolle, and Strachan. Thus, operating within the Bahamas limits the potential for Haitian social advancement.[10] Bahamians fear that Haitians threaten Bahamian sovereignty and prosperity though, in fact, Haitians partly facilitate Bahamian prosperity due to the way in which their labor is exploited in the Bahamian economy. Haitian Protestant migrants and their progeny turn to their religious practices to provide a *bourad* (boost) in a country that rejects and scapegoats them (see Rey and Stepick 2010). Their religious culture and practices also offer them a model for how to conduct themselves in this foreign country.

Theory

At the heart of the shift in religious practice toward Protestantism in the Bahamas is a distinction-making process devout migrants use to differentiate themselves from other migrants. The process reflects how they survive in the Bahamas and how they reimagine Haiti as a Protestant Christian nation. The majority of my research consultants used three major categories—*Kretyen*, *Pwotestan*, and *moun ki poko konvèti* (people who have not converted to a Protestant form of Christianity)—to differentiate themselves from one another. By understanding why devout Protestant migrants use these terms and what their ramifications are, we can gain insights into both the shift to Protestantism as the majority religion practiced by Haitians in the Bahamas and the broader success of evangelical Protestantism in Latin America and the Caribbean, areas of the world that used to be Catholic strongholds.

This book argues that some devout Haitian Protestants in the Bahamas use the terms *Pwotestan* and *moun ki poko konvèti* as moral critiques of how Protestant Christianity is practiced by other Haitian migrants. Their use of the term *Kretyen* reflects their beliefs that the "authentic" practice of Haitian Protestantism will improve the lives of Haitians in the Bahamas and in Haiti. When Haitian Protestants in the Bahamas privately refer to other people in their churches and the larger migrant community as *Pwotestan* and *moun ki poko konvèti*, they are judging individuals whom they consider to be at the root of the problems that affect Haitians in the Bahamas because they are not *Kretyen*, that is, authentic Christians who fear God and behave in a manner that contributes to the betterment of Haiti. In this sense *Kretyen* can be understood as a religious identity and also as a form of nationalist expression that is used to combat marginalization in the Bahamas. In the context of a transnational social field that includes the Bahamas, Haiti, and the United States, those who view themselves as *Kretyen* in the Bahamas believe that Haiti's socioeconomic, ecological, and environmental crises stem from moral and spiritual problems among the Haitian citizenry and state. The use of these differentiating terms thus highlights how diaspora, migration, nationalism, and transnationalism are intertwined as migrants recreate and practice Haitian Protestant Christianity in the Bahamas and conceptualize their religious and political milieu.

To analyze the distinction-making process of devout Haitian Protestant migrants, this book employs the concept of symbolic boundaries, as articulated by sociologist Michele Lamont (1992). Lamont and sociologist Virag Molnar (2002, 187) write that "the notion of boundaries is crucial for analyzing how social actors construct groups as similar and different and how it shapes their understanding of their responsibilities toward such groups." This book analyzes how different social groups in New Providence, Bahamas—Bahamians, Haitian Protestants, and Bahamians of Haitian descent—define themselves through their use of symbolic boundaries. It also illustrates how symbolic boundaries are formed, how they are used on an everyday basis, and how they provide a foundation for the reimagination of Haiti as a Protestant Christian nation.

When Bahamians deem that Haitians are a "burden" to the Bahamas and perceive Haitians as taxing Bahamian social services and hospitals, and "fixing" Bahamians (casting spells to harm Bahamians and, by extension, the Bahamas), they draw polarizing ethnic boundaries that marginalize people of Haitian descent, legitimate anti-Haitian discrimination in Bahamian society, and foster a social order that is structured to maintain a permanent Haitian underclass. When devout Haitian Protestant migrants believe that their religious community is dysfunctional and in "complete chaos," they draw symbolic boundaries between themselves and other Haitian migrants that criticize community behavior and the practice of Protestant forms of Christianity in the Bahamas. By understanding why these different social groups use symbolic boundaries, we can learn more about how Bahamian society is structured, how devout Haitian Protestants try to recreate Protestant forms of Christianity as they were practiced in Haiti, and why deep inequalities persist in the Caribbean. Moreover, by focusing on the religious activities and observations of Haitian Protestants in New Providence, this book demonstrates why some Haitian Protestants employ a conceptual continuum of moral purity—consisting of *Kretyen, Pwotestan,* and *moun ki poko konvèti*—and why these identities have risen to prominence among devout migrants. The use of this conceptual continuum is important because it demonstrates how migrants create meaning out of their religious experience rather than copying Christian practices in their host country for utilitarian reasons, such as procuring employment and advancing in Bahamian society.

In this ethnography I draw on the work of anthropologists who counter, as anthropologist Fenella Cannell (2006) writes, a widespread, although not total, disciplinary bias in the study of Christianity within anthropology. Cannell (2006, 3) observes that some scholars take a "secular analytical approach" to the study of Christianity while others sometimes seem "exaggeratedly resistant to the possibility of taking seriously the religious experiences of others." When analyzing conversion to Christianity in the lives of people living in the underdeveloped world, previous anthropological studies that used the "secular analytical approach" have attributed Christianity to factors other than the people's attempts to understand the world around them and their existence through a religious framework that is usually foreign to them. For example, religious conversion to Christianity by the Tswana of South Africa was not viewed as an attempt to restructure their world but as the result of intense missionary efforts, backed by colonial and Western powers (Comaroff and

Comaroff 1991). In reaction to views that evangelical growth in Latin America is solely the result of forces from the United States, anthropologist David Stoll (1990, xvi) opines that to see the conversion to Christianity as less than cultural "suggests a deep distrust of the poor, an unwillingness to accept the possibility that they could turn an imported religion to their own purposes."

In response to this hegemonic view of Christianity within anthropology, anthropologists such as Webb Keane (2007), Fenella Cannell (2006), Susan Harding (1991; 1987; 2000), Brian Howell (2007), and Joel Robbins (2004a; 2004b) have contributed greatly to the advancement of the study of the practice of Christianity by viewing the practice of Christianity as cultural. I draw on their work in my own analysis of devout Haitian Protestant migrants. Specifically, I employ an intellectualist approach to analyze the discourse of Haitian Protestant migrants who construct themselves as *Kretyen*. This approach emphasizes why people convert and how they make meaning out of religion (Robbins 2004a).

Using an intellectualist approach is necessary in conducting an ethnography about Haitian Protestant Christianity due to the huge imbalance in the scholarly literature about the religions Haitians practice. Anthropologists and religious studies experts traditionally have paid more attention to the study of Vodou and Catholicism among Haitians and less attention to the Haitian practice of Protestant Christianity. While influential texts, such as *Mama Lola* by anthropologist Karen McCarthy Brown and *The Faces of the Gods* by anthropologist Leslie Desmangles, were written to challenge Western stereotypes about the practice of New World African religions like Vodou, a traditional research focus on Catholicism and Vodou has ignored contemporary Haitian religious practices and the growing number of Protestant Christians in Haiti and in diasporic contexts such as Canada, the Bahamas, the Dominican Republic, Guadeloupe, and the United States. When some scholarly attention is devoted to the study of Haitian Protestantism, it tends to emphasize utilitarian explanations for its existence and spread among Haitians (Métraux 1958; Richman 2005a). Although utilitarian motives

may motivate some Haitians to convert to Protestant forms of Christianity, many Haitian Protestants develop a worldview that is intellectualist
in its foundation.

The intellectualist approach also helps to illuminate my research consultants' responses: how they described themselves, their faith, and their
opinions of other Haitian Protestants within their religious community. It
helps to articulate why Haitians remain Protestant—rather than switching between Protestantism, Catholicism, and Vodou—and why they
draw the symbolic boundaries of *Kretyen*, *Pwotestan*, and *moun ki poko
konvèti*. And it enables us to understand the interviewees' comments as
a critique of their churches and religious community.

This book also applies the theoretical lens of transnationalism—as
informed by transnational migration literature (see Basch et al. 1994;
Tsuda 2003; Rouse 1991) and transnational religious migration literature
(Ebaugh and Chafetz 2002; Mooney 2009; Richman 2005a)—to interpret
the religious lives of Haitian Protestants in the Bahamas. Transnationalism helps to explain processes that immigrants use to forge and sustain
multistranded social relations that connect societies of origin and settlement (Basch et al. 1994). It is linked to the changing conditions of global
capitalism and must be analyzed in terms of global relations between
capital and labor. Transnational relationships create social fields that go
beyond national boundaries. Bounded social scientific concepts that con-
flate physical location, culture, and identity limit the ability of researchers
to perceive and analyze transnational phenomena. Transmigrants—people whose identities are split between two or more nations, such as the
devout Haitian Protestant migrants discussed in this book—find themselves confronted with and engaged in the nation-building processes of
two or more nation-states. Their identities and practices are configured
and constructed according to hegemonic categories, such as race and
ethnicity, which are deeply embedded in the nation-building processes
of multiple nation-states (Basch et al. 1994). My research consultants'
experiences are situated within the Bahamas and a larger, transnational
social field that includes Haiti and the United States. It is insufficient to

study the comments, opinions, rituals, and religious beliefs of Haitian Protestants in the Bahamas solely by attending to the physical boundaries of the Bahamian nation-state because their identities exceed such boundaries. A transnational social field is also the larger context where my research about Haitian Protestantism took place.

Methods

Before studying the migrant practice of Protestant Christianity in the Bahamas, I participated in familial religious activities in the United States and Haiti, observed and interviewed research participants at Haitian Protestant churches in the greater Saint Louis, Missouri area, and conducted fieldwork in Haiti in Protestant milieus. The majority of my mother's nuclear and extended family was raised in Haiti's Protestant Christian movement. Her mother, Alice Fougy (née Alice Jean Louis), was an evangelist who would preach the gospel of Jesus Christ throughout Haiti and in Haitian diasporic communities in Massachusetts (Boston), New York (New York City, Spring Valley), and the Washington, DC area. In my youth, my mother would bring me to services at one of the first Haitian Baptist churches in New York City, L'Église Baptiste d'Éxpression Française (French Speaking Baptist Church), located in Brooklyn. We would participate in Actions de Graces à L'Éternel (Thanksgiving)—which included worship and praise of the Lord, testimonials, impromptu sermons, and a call for nonbelievers to accept Jesus Christ as their savior—with maternal relatives in Boston, the Washington, DC area, and Spring Valley, New York.[11]

After participating and observing festivities and services at Haitian Protestant churches (two Baptist, one nondenominational) in Saint Peters, Saint Louis, and Kansas City, Missouri, I wanted to learn more about the socio-religious context that produced Haitian Protestant immigrants in the United States. In summer 2002 I traveled to Haiti for six weeks to research various aspects of Haitian Protestant church life and culture. I employed semistructured and structured interviews and

participant observation of various Haitian Protestant events and rituals. One of the main events on my research trip to Haiti was an Actions
de Grâces, which was performed on July 25, 2002, in Ti Rivye (or Little
River, "Petite Rivière" in French), an agrarian village located outside of
Jacmel in the Southwestern department of Haiti. Ti Rivye was the birth-
place of my grandmother and the Actions de Grâces was held in honor
of the exemplary Christian life she had led. When she died in October
2001, one of her last wishes was that her family would not forget their
relatives in Ti Rivye. Members of my immediate and extended families
as well as members of the Boston Missionary Baptist Church, including
my uncle, the Reverend Dr. Soliny Védrine, who would be instrumental
in connecting me with pastors in the Bahamas, attended the event.[12]

I arrived in New Providence, Bahamas, in February 2005, and divided
my research among three Haitian Protestant churches: New Haitian Mission Baptist Church (New Mission), Victory Chapel Church of the Nazarene, and International Tabernacle of Praise Ministries, Incorporated
(an interdenominational church). Upon my arrival, I spent my time
at New Mission participating in Sunday services and *lajènes* (church
youth group) meetings. In July 2005 I began interviewing people at New
Mission and the other two churches. Based on research questions and
assumptions about what I would find when I started my field interviews,
I used what is known as a purposive or judgment sample. When using
this type of sampling technique, one defines the purpose one wants
one's research consultants to serve and then looks for consultants who
meet those characteristics (Bernard 2002, 182).[13] I used this technique
because in the early stages of interviewing I wanted to study people
who had switched denominations. Having identified the first group of
people—Haitians who had left Catholicism and converted to Protestantism—through activities at New Haitian Mission Baptist Church, I used
an interview protocol that elicited detailed responses about educational
background, family dynamics, family traditions, religious development,
church affiliations, work histories, life in the Bahamas, and views of Haiti,
Haitian society, my informants' future, and the future of Haiti. Although

my sample was not representative, the comments from the participants revealed a lot about Haitian Protestant churches in the Bahamas, Bahamian church culture, and the tensions between Haitians and children of Haitian descent living in the Bahamas. Their comments also uncovered the meaning of the terms *Kretyen*, *Pwotestan*, and *moun ki poko konvèti*, and what anthropologist Takeyuki Tsuda (2003, 27) refers to as the "honne" in Japan: private information that includes personal opinions, private attitudes, and inner feelings hidden from public view.

I primarily used open-ended questions that allowed respondents to interpret the questions and elaborate on their answers; for example, "What is your opinion of the Haitian Protestant community in New Providence? What do you like about it and what do you not like about it?" The first interviews were tested with Bahamian and immigrant research consultants. After those interviews, I interviewed seven Haitians from International Tabernacle of Praise Ministries and New Haitian Mission Baptist Church. I began interviewing in July 2005 and finished in December 2005. Yet, it was not until Dieunous Senatus, assistant pastor of Victory Chapel, described the difference between migrants who practiced Protestant Christianity in a devout manner and other Protestant migrants who still committed egregious sins, that I decided to alter my interview protocol.[14] Specifically, I determined that asking about the general differences between a *Pwotestan* and a *Kretyen* would be another interesting question to pose to informants while I gathered data about religious choice and denominational change. As it happened, the distinction that devout migrants made between *Kretyen* and *Pwotestan* caused me to disregard my original research agenda and became the focus of this book.

From that point forward I modified the interview protocol to include questions that teased out distinctions concerning religious and ethnic identities among Haitians and Bahamians of Haitian descent.[15] For instance, in the section of the interview schedule about religious development and affiliation I asked research consultants to describe the difference between a Haitian Protestant and a Haitian Catholic, explain the difference between a Protestant in Haiti and a Haitian Protestant in

New Providence, and describe the difference between a Haitian Protestant and a Haitian Christian.[16] I interviewed members of each church,
including two migrant men who attended two additional Haitian Protestant churches not featured in the ethnography, one migrant woman
who worked at the place where I stayed, and a Bahamian man of Haitian
descent who practices Catholicism. I collected five preliminary interviews from four Haitians and one Trinidadian who helped me to develop
questions for a protocol for in-depth interviews. In total, I collected fifty-
three in-depth interviews from Bahamians (five), Haitians (thirty-six),
and Bahamians of Haitian descent (ten), as well as from two non-Haitian
immigrants—one Trinidadian and the other Canadian. Out of the thirty-
six Haitian Protestants I interviewed, seventeen were not asked about the
Pwotestan/Kretyen distinction because I had not yet interviewed Pastor
Senatus; thus, the new focus on this distinction was to be developed.
Eighteen of the research consultants noted a difference between a *Pwotestan* and a *Kretyen*, attributing negative qualities to *Pwotestans* and positive ones to *Kretyens*. One person I interviewed declined to answer those
questions when they were posed to her.

   In addition to formal interviewing, I was a participant observer in the
religious lives of my research consultants. Participant observers can be
insiders who observe some aspects of life around them, or they can be
outsiders who participate in some aspects of life around them and take
notes or record what they see and hear (Bernard 2002, 327). While in
New Providence, I attended a variety of services at the three dominant
churches featured in this book as well as other Bahamian and Haitian
churches. Since each church held morning and evening services on Sundays, I could visit more than one church on a given day. At the services
I would sing hymns (in Haitian Creole, French, and English), pray, take
pictures of church activities, and film portions of the services. I spent
the first five months in New Providence at New Mission, splitting my
remaining time in the Bahamas between International Tabernacle of
Praise and Victory Chapel Church of the Nazarene. I also attended Bible
study and *lajènes* meetings at the churches.

Participating in church activities throughout the week enhanced my Haitian Protestant habitus (behaving, speaking, worshipping, praying, and carrying myself as an adherent of Protestant Christianity would), which I had developed during fieldwork among Haitian Protestants in Saint Louis, Missouri, and Haiti. My time spent at *lajènes* meetings at New Mission and Victory Chapel helped the members become more comfortable around me. It also gave me access to a large pool of interview participants, even though they were initially aloof and treated me like an outsider. At Victory Chapel Church of the Nazarene, it was only after I shared my experiences of racism and alienation in the public school system in New York City that Bahamians of Haitian descent, who felt discriminated against by Bahamians in their school system, opened up to me in interviews. Teaching an English class to adherents at International Tabernacle of Praise broke the ice and allowed me to interview people I could not have had access to otherwise because of their suspicions about my religious identity and their doubts about whether I was a person whom they could trust with their private information.

My observations contributed to this study in different ways. By participating in and observing Haitian Protestant rituals and practices in Sunday school, *jènn* (prayer services), Sunday morning and evening services, Bible study, choir rehearsals, and interdenominational meetings, I could discern how someone could easily learn the rules of proper appearance and comportment within the church. Furthermore, based on the way men and women carried themselves within the walls and outside the walls of their churches, as well as the rigid categories that participants constructed in their interviews, I also was able to discern how Haitian Protestants could be categorized as either *Pwotestan* or *Kretyen*. In other words, there were moments in the field when, through my observations of and discussions with my research consultants, I could determine whether they had reoriented their worldview according to devout Haitian Protestant beliefs and traditions or viewed the world in a manner that was antithetical to that religious culture.

After attending services at all three churches numerous times—playing the role of cultural outsider that anthropologist Clifford Geertz (1973) describes in his classic essay "Deep Play: Notes on the Balinese Cockfight," and improving my linguistic competency in Haitian Creole—adherents at all churches began to speak more freely to me. When I finally interviewed people, they helped me see beyond the surface of rituals that lead casual observers of Haitian Protestantism to homogenize this transnational religious movement into a religion that is practiced the same way by Haitians virtually everywhere. When I started recording my first interview I began a journey that took me into a vast and complex world where migration, ethnicity, religious practice, ideology, nationalism, asceticism, candid comments, and hope and despair were all intertwined to illuminate a world few people outside of Haiti and Haitian communities knew existed. This book describes that world and how the use of symbolic boundaries by devout Haitian Protestant migrants expresses a critique of the Haitian practice of Protestantism in the Bahamas as well as a critique of citizenship in Haiti that is intended to solve Haiti's crisis and realize a Protestant Christian Haiti that is respected among other nations.

The Organization of the Book

To understand the religious practice of Haitian migrants, it is necessary to learn more about the type of Protestantism they used to practice in Haiti. Chapter 1 covers the culture of Haitian Protestantism with a focus on its shared aspects emphasized by migrants. Chapter 2 introduces the island of New Providence and explains how Haitian migration to the Bahamas and Bahamian laws combine to exploit and marginalize Haitian life there. Chapter 3 discusses the Haitian Protestant community of New Providence as seen by the pastors at the respective churches featured in this book and the transnational Haitian Protestant elements at play within the community. Chapter 4 examines Haitian Protestant liturgy and focuses on how worship and praise combine with Haitian Protestant hymnody and sermons to encourage migrants to lead Christian lives. Chapter 5 analyzes the categories of *Kretyen, Pwotestan,* and *moun ki poko konvèti* to reveal their meanings within the boundaries of the Bahamian nation-state and a larger transnational context that includes Haiti. The conclusion revisits the idea of modernity as it is expressed among Haitian Protestant migrants in relation to Haitians in the Bahamas and the future of Haiti. It also highlights this book's theoretical contributions to the scholarship of the anthropology of Christianity, Haitian studies, religious studies and the understanding of the success of evangelical forms of Christianity in Latin America and the Caribbean. But this ethnography begins with an embarrassing experience I had during fieldwork in Haiti that helped me to understand the importance of appearance and comportment as it relates to Haitian Protestant culture and identity in the Bahamas.

1

Haitian Protestant Culture

"Why do you wear your hair like that? You should have hair like me!" These were the words of a pastor admonishing me while I was being threatened with physical removal from a Pentecostal church in Port-au-Prince, Haiti, in 2002.[1] I had gone to Haiti to study Protestant religious culture, seeking to understand how it affected the lives of Haitian Protestant migrants. I would learn that the religious culture of Protestants in Haiti directly informs the production of symbolic boundaries by Haitian Protestant migrants in the United States and the Bahamas. As anthropologist Takeyuki Tsuda argues, a complete and comprehensive ethnography of the lives of transmigrants (people whose identities are split between two or more nation-states) requires fieldwork in both the sending country and the receiving country to understand the influence of migration on their ethnicity and to analyze the transnational linkages between the two countries that frame their experiences (Tsuda 2003, 55). Without sufficient knowledge of the premigratory religious experiences of Protestant Christians in Haiti, any analysis of the post migratory experiences in the Bahamas would be religiously decontextualized.

From July to August 2002 I participated in and observed church services and other Protestant practices in Port-au-Prince. During this time I wore my hair in dreadlocks, a hairstyle in which strands of hair are twisted into ropelike locks. While walking down the streets of Port-au-Prince I, a black American of Haitian descent, was referred to as a *blan* (white; foreigner) and "dred." I was unfamiliar with the religious culture of Protestant churches in Haiti and did not anticipate that the way I wore my hair would be a problem. The reactions I received to wearing dread-locks in the United States were more of a complimentary nature and it was also a common hairstyle for men and women of African descent in Saint Louis, Missouri, where I lived at that time. In fact, I was not made to feel uncomfortable at the Haitian Protestant churches I had attended previously in Kansas City and Saint Louis, Missouri, New York, and Boston, Massachusetts. So I naïvely believed that my hair and my presence, by extension, would not be an issue, let alone a spectacle, in a Protestant church in Port-au-Prince.

While in Port-au-Prince, I spent the majority of my time at the First Baptist Church of Port-au-Prince, and I recall receiving some stares from other churchgoers the first few times I attended Sunday morning services. At a later visit, an elderly churchwoman told me that it is written in the Holy Bible that men should not wear their hair long. One of my cousins, with whom I went to that church regularly, leapt to my defense and demanded to know where in the Holy Bible the biblical law admonishing men with long hair can be found. My accuser could not recall. I would later find out that the Bible verse with which the woman attempted to discipline me could be found in 1 Corinthians 1:14–15 (Ryrie Study Bible 1994, 1768), which states: "Does not the very nature of things teach you that if a man has long hair, it is a disgrace to him, but that if a woman has long hair, it is her glory?" The next time my dreadlocks became an issue was at a Pentecostal church.

Since my exposure to Protestantism in Haiti during the trip had been limited to Adventists and Baptists, I decided to attend a Pentecostal service one Sunday to broaden my perspective. My maternal aunt agreed to accompany me and we attended service at L'Église de Dieu (Church of God), Delmas in Port-au-Prince. I began filming the service without prior approval from a church official. Twenty minutes into the service a church member approached me and demanded to know who I was, why I was filming, and whether I had received authorization from the head pastor. I explained the nature of my research and we walked down to the bottom level of the church to receive authorization. The head pastor

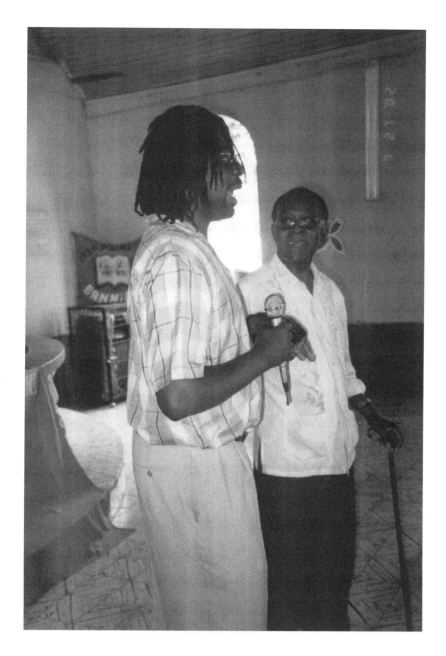

The author, with his father, Bertin Louis, MD, addressing the congregation at L'Église de Saint Paul, Port-au-Prince, Haiti, July 2002.

immediately interrogated me while church congregants surrounded us. He asked me: "Why do wear your hair like that? You should have hair like me! [He wore his hair in a well-kept Afro.] Are you converted? We don't allow people like you in our church!" I apologized profusely about filming church activities without prior approval and explained that I was an anthropology doctoral student studying Protestantism in Haiti. The main reason that I was not physically removed from the church that day was the fact that I am also the grandson of Alice Jean-Louis Fougy, a renowned Haitian Baptist missionary who had preached in Haiti and throughout the Haitian diaspora for more than fifty years and who had passed away in 2001. The head pastor had known her personally, and after I informed him of my relationship to her, he agreed that it would be fine for me to continue to film the service. When I rejoined the service he made an announcement in front of his congregation of three hundred to four hundred people that I would be filming at the church that day. He added, "Please do not be shocked by his appearance."

After this mortifying experience, I learned that in order to conduct research among Protestants in Haiti and elsewhere, I needed to cut off my long hair (which I did in 2004) and wear it in an appropriate manner for conducting fieldwork among Haitian adherents of Protestant Christianity. Being accosted by a church lady at one church, and being threatened with removal by a pastor from another, has taught me a great deal about Haitian Protestantism. Appearance—that is, the way Haitian Protestant Christian men and women dress, wear their hair, and present themselves in public—is one of the shared aspects of Haitian Protestant culture that provides the burgeoning transnational religious movement with some cohesion. That I was made to feel uncomfortable because of the way I wore my hair, then, is linked to the creation and maintenance of Protestant Christian religious boundaries in Haiti and the Haitian diaspora. Throughout my time in Haiti and the Bahamas, it became readily apparent that appearance in Haitian Protestantism is a reflection of *karacktè* (character), a fundamental and foundational trait of someone who comes from the devout Haitian Protestant Christian tradition. In the

Bahamas, appearance was a key factor in the creation and maintenance of the symbolic boundaries (*Kretyen, Pwotestan,* and *moun ki poko konvèti*) that organize parts of the archipelago's Haitian Protestant diaspora. The reactions to my appearance from Pentecostals in Haiti were similar to the reactions I observed and recorded in interviews among devout migrants in the Bahamas to seemingly less devout Protestants. These reactions reflect Protestant Christian culture in Haiti, which is the starting point for Haitian migrant religious practice in New Providence. My transnational research demonstrates that the appearance of migrants is an aspect of a larger, shared religious culture that is maintained and emphasized in the Bahamas. Another factor that gives this transnational religious movement some cohesion is the Protestant Christian rejection of Vodou.

Rejection of Vodou as a Unifying Factor

Haitian Protestantism, as scholars have noted, defines itself in relation to Vodou. When Protestantism made inroads in Haiti during François Duvalier's dictatorship (1957–1971), many Haitians who previously had served *lwa* (ancestral spirits) publicly renounced them and became Protestant. As Frederick Conway (1978, 169), an American anthropologist who wrote one of the first ethnographies about Haitian Pentecostalism recognizes, "the fine theological distinctions which separate the various Protestant denominations are not particularly meaningful to Haitians. That all Protestant organizations oppose Vodou and promise protection to those who reject Vodou is more significant." This stance against Vodou is also prevalent among Haitian Protestants in the Bahamas. When migrants in New Providence's Protestant community were asked why so many Haitians are poor, why there were high rates of unemployment in Haiti, and why the Haitian economy is in shambles, most respondents considered an overarching spiritual factor that is at the heart of Haiti's troubles in general and has affected their personal lives in the Bahamas as well: Vodou. Many devout Haitian Protestant migrants pinpoint the exact historical moment when Haiti's misfortune began to the *Bwa Kayiman*

(Bois Caïman) Vodou Congress, which, as noted earlier, occurred in the French colony of Saint-Domingue when Haitians are said to have received their freedom from European colonial powers through consecration with *dyab* (the Devil). A maroon who escaped from a plantation near Morne Rouge named Boukman led the *Bwa Kayiman* Vodou Congress, which was pivotal to the beginning of the Haitian Revolution (1791–1803). Trinidadian Marxist historian C. L. R. James (1963, 87) observed the importance of this moment in a stirring account of the ceremony, believed to have occurred in August 1791:

> A tropical storm raged, with lightning and gusts of wind and heavy showers of rain. . . . [T]here Boukman gave the last instructions and, after Vodou incantations and the sucking of the blood of a stuck pig, he stimulated his followers by a prayer spoken in creole, which, like so much spoken on such occasions, has remained. "The god who created the sun which gives us light, who rouses the waves and rules the storm, though hidden in the clouds, he watches us. He sees all that the white man does. The god of the white man inspires us with crime, but our god calls upon us to do good works. Our god who is good to us orders us to revenge out wrongs. He will direct our arms and aid us. Throw away the symbol of the god of the whites who has caused us to weep, and listen to the voices of liberty, which speaks in the hearts of us all."

Six days later, slaves of the Turpin plantation, led by Boukman, indiscriminately massacred every white man, woman, and child they could find (Simpson 1945). This event began a general insurrection that would lead to the Haitian Revolution, the only successful slave revolt in human history that extended the rights of liberty, brotherhood, and equality to black people and articulated common humanity and equality for all Haitian citizens.

Although the story of *Bwa Kayiman* has inspired many Haitians and other peoples of African descent who share a similar history of bondage, many Haitian Protestants today find it offensive and believe that this event was the exact historical moment when Haiti was "consecrated to the Devil." By extension, then, *Bwa Kayiman* is seen to have ensured a legacy of misery in Haiti that is reflected by the underdevelopment that grips it today.

This counter-hegemonic reading of *Bwa Kayiman* is clearly articulated by Chavannes Jeune, a pastor and evangelist from Les Cayes, Haiti who was a candidate for the Haitian presidency in 2005. He is also the president of the Baptist Church of Southern Haiti and the founder of a group called "Haiti for the Third Century" that has as its purpose to "take Haiti back from the Devil, and dedicate her to Jesus Christ." In an interview with the *Lincoln Tribune*, Pastor Chavannes stated his belief that the nation of Haiti is still in bondage primarily because "the country was dedicated by a Vodou priest [Boukman] at its liberation" and "[Haiti] has been in bondage to the Devil for four generations" (Barrick 2005).

While Haitian Protestants acknowledge that Vodou is part of Haitian culture and their *rasin* (roots), it is supposed to be rejected by a Protestant Christian. Dr. Charles Poisset Romain, a Haitian sociologist and the preeminent expert on Haitian Protestantism, explains that Protestantism is a religion of rupture. This rupture occurs with *lemonn* (the secular world) and the rejection of Vodou, a New World African religion, and is essential to being modern and to being a Christian (1986, 2004).

In interviews conducted with devout Haitian Protestant migrants in the Bahamas, I asked two questions concerning Haiti and contemporary Haitian society. The first question was *"Sò panse de sitiasyon sosyal Ayiti* (What do you think of Haiti's social situation)?" and the second *"Sò panse Ayiti bezwen pou chanje sitiasyon sosyal li* (What do you think Haiti needs to change its current situation)?" In response to the first question, the majority of respondents born and raised in Haiti described the country's situation in overwhelmingly negative terms.[2] One Haitian Protestant male, who stayed in contact with family and friends in Haiti during the time of his interview, stated that he had heard that life in Haiti had worsened since he left for New Providence in 2002. When the second question was answered, the majority of respondents referred to God as the only solution to both alleviate Haiti's endemic poverty and stabilize this country racked by economic, social, and political crises. Many also averred that if the country's president was a devout Protestant Christian, the country would have a better future. Sister Maude's reflections illuminate this common belief that the practice of Vodou is an important reason behind the crisis in Haiti.

I interviewed Sister Maude in New Providence on September 6, 2005, about her life and her views on Haitian Protestantism. At the time of our interview, she was thirty-one years old and had attended International Tabernacle of Praise Ministries for one year. She had converted to Protestantism when she was thirteen and was baptized at age seventeen. Unlike the majority of Haitians who migrate to the Bahamas from Haiti's northern states, she was from Port-au-Prince, Haiti's capital. Before her migration she had attended L'Église Baptiste Patriarche de Caseau, a charismatic Baptist church in Port-au-Prince where adherents receive the gifts of the Holy Spirit. In her interview, she explained that her family was deep into Vodou, and she listed different family members who served *lwa*.

I asked Sister Maude to describe Haiti's socioeconomic situation at the time. She replied, "I don't see anything for Haiti. For Haiti to change its current situation, the people have to stop committing crimes, stop the blood from running in the streets, and turn their faces toward God. Turn their faces toward God because the people, the Haitian people, have consecrated the country with the Devil."[3] When asked further about her opinion of Vodou and its effects on Haitian society, she attested:

> Haitians give Vodou top place in Haitian society. . . . It's the reason why the country is in the state it's in, you understand what I'm saying?
>
> Imagine a person, a small peasant who [has not enough to eat for himself] but has a goat, and is feeding it, fattening it up to give to *lwa* (ancestral spirits), to give *lwa* food every year. While this person is fattening the goat, this person has children, this person has who knows how many children they can't send to school. And then this person has to save what

they have to give *lwa* food. What is this person giving their food to? Some talking [incantations], something this person does [rituals associated with Vodou], and then throws the stuff on the floor? Imagine a person who goes to a sacred tree every year and then rolls around in the mud, a place that's dirty, a place that smells like a place where a pig would roll around in. How can you make me understand [this] . . . that this is not misery that the Devil is creating in the country?

Do you understand what I'm saying? Because if you're not a pig there's no reason for you to be rolling around in the mud. How does someone bathe in dirty water, in mud? The person is not a pig. This is normal for a pig. . . . I think that all of our ignorance, [the ignorance of] the Haitian people, causes the country to be in the state that it's in. For there to be true change in Haiti there needs to be no less than everyone saying, "Okay, I renounce all of the worthless *lwa*, all of the worthless saints, all of the worthless statues" . . . and well, turn their faces toward God and that's when God will say something on their behalf. But as long as they continue to give *lwa* food, worship sacred trees, make a bunch of faces, the country will never change. Instead of changing [for the better] it will get worse. . . . That means that a president will never be able to change it. . . . Only God can change [our situation].⁴

Sister Maude's statements, made five years before the January 12, 2010, Haiti earthquake, mirror those of Pat Robertson and other devout Haitian Protestants. She interprets Haiti's crisis as a spiritual crisis that can only be transformed through the catalytic action of the Holy Spirit. She contrasts her fundamentalist religious beliefs with the assumed deleterious effects of Vodou on Haitian citizens, demonstrating her belief that Vodou encourages ignorance and waste. Consequently, in her view, the transformation of Haiti into a safe and stable nation-state can occur only through the conversion of the entire Haitian populace to Protestant forms of Christianity.

Sister Ann, a Haitian woman in her twenties at the time of our interview, shared similar views regarding Vodou and Haiti. She attended

New Haitian Mission Baptist Church in New Providence, taught Sunday school, and participated in *lajènes*. She was a Catholic before she converted to Protestantism at a Baptist crusade in her teens and had attended a charismatic Baptist church in Haiti's Northwestern department for two years before she migrated to the Bahamas. A belief shared by many Haitians, regardless of religious affiliation is that *maji* (magic, sorcery) can be used against one's enemies. This belief was apparent in Sister Ann's description of an incident at New Haitian Mission Baptist Church:

> People from Haiti . . . , all Haitians . . . say that if Protestants have a disagreement with someone, they say that Protestant will go to the Vodou priest's house to "fix" that person. Here in Nassau, Protestants say they'll "go to Haiti" for the person.[5] For example, a woman had a problem with another person at the church and in front of the woman, in front of the church, she said, *"M prale Ayiti pou ou"* (I'm going to Haiti to "fix" you).

Sister Ann then grabbed a photo album and flipped through the pages. While she was looking she said:

> [This woman] told [another woman] that she's going to Haiti, she'll have her killed by going to Haiti. . . . [S]he's going to Haiti to have her killed [She finds a picture and shows it to me] . . . . the mother of this young woman.
>
> This is a Haitian problem, it's not a problem Haitians have because of Nassau. The person said she's Protestant but she has a problem with someone, she says to the person "I'm Protestant but my father isn't." This means that she has a spirit to do evil things, to steal, things like that."[6]

Sister Ann's comments illuminate another perceived deleterious effect of Vodou: promoting death. Vodou is believed to be a religion of the Devil in which its followers pray to idols that imbue them with spirits of evil. The disciplined practice of authentic Protestant Christianity, then, is seen to be not only the logical religious choice for any Haitian concerning his or her personal salvation but also for ensuring a positive future for Haiti. Many devout Haitian Protestant Christians believe that conversion to and authentic practice of Protestant forms of Christianity will teach fellow Haitians to love each other, inspired by passages from the Holy Bible.[7] They see Vodou as teaching one to hate one's neighbor by working for their downfall by using *maji* against them. Vodou is, in the imagination of many Haitian Protestants, a religious "culture of poverty," an adaptation to a set of objective conditions transmitted from generation to generation, keeping Haitians and Haiti from developing into a modern, civilized, and spiritually liberated nation.

Protestant Vocabulary and Practice as Unifying Factors

Because many devout Haitian Protestants share the view that many of Haiti's spiritual and moral problems are rooted in the practice of Vodou, conversion is seen as a starting point for the transformation of the individual and then the collective and spiritual needs of Haiti will follow. Dr. Antoine Saint Louis, head pastor of Victory Chapel Church of the Nazarene, preached a sermon on September 11, 2005, from the book of Genesis 32:22–32.[8] This sermon dealt with conversion and also utilized some of the vocabulary that is shared among adherents in Haitian Protestant churches on the island of New Providence. Dr. Saint Louis's sermon discussed what a Protestant God changes in a person. According to the sermon, God challenged Jacob, and changed his name to Israel and then everything about Jacob changed. Pastor Saint Louis then drew parallels between what happened to Jacob and what happens to Haitians when they decide to convert to Protestant Christianity. For example, like Jacob's name change, Haitian Protestants also experience a name change when they address each other as *frè* (brother) or *sè* (sister) after conversion. Furthermore, one's comportment—or what Haitian Protestants call one's *mach* that reflects how one represents oneself to *lemonn* (the secular world) through behavior and appearance—changes when one converts and matures in one's new faith.

While many devout Haitian Protestants throughout the community in New Providence use the term *Christian* to describe themselves, some Haitian Catholics are included as perceived *Kretyens* because they do not mix Vodou and Catholicism in their religious practices (those who do are known as *Katolik fran*). Haitian Catholics in New Providence, though, are usually lumped into the category of *moun ki poko konvèti* by devout migrants. In the eyes of these migrants, involvement in *legliz Babilon* (the Babylonian church) essentially means involvement in a corrupt church.

Anthropologist Frederick Conway's dissertation on Pentecostalism and health in Haiti reveals another important aspect in understanding why Haitian Protestants do not always consider Haitian Catholics to be Christians. When asked to identify his or her religion, Conway notes that the Vodouist will respond Catholic, because there is little real distinction made between Catholicism and Vodou (Conway 1978, 54). In order to appease *lwa*, one must know Catholic rituals and rites. In Haitian Protestantism there is only one God. The relationship of Haitian Catholicism to Vodou is complex while the relationship of Haitian Protestantism to Vodou is simple in that Haitian Protestants theoretically reject and do not practice Vodou.

Aside from the *pastè* (pastor), an assistant pastor, *dyak* (a deacon), and ushers, the congregation of Haitian Protestant churches is made up of two types of people: *manm legliz* (church member) and *kwayan* (believer). Members of a church are different from believers in that they usually have been baptized. Baptism in most Haitian Protestant churches is the full immersion in water of an adult by a minister. Baptism is a rite of passage in Protestant Christianity, which symbolizes *yon dèzyem nesans*, the rebirth of a person into someone new. At a baptism in New Providence on October 16, 2005, a pastor assisting Pastor Kevin Pierre, head pastor of International Tabernacle of Praise Ministries, in the baptism of five church members described baptism as *angajman de konsyan*, a conscious commitment or decision that must be taken seriously.[9]

When one is baptized, one is supposed to proceed with the ritual with a clear commitment to Christ, which translates to a clear conscience. The life of a Christian within the Haitian Protestant community of New Providence requires living out the beliefs that are preached by evangelists, pastors, and missionaries. After the baptism one should demonstrate a complete transformation in one's behavior, comportment, language, and habits; that is, a person who smokes cigarettes, drinks alcohol, uses profanity, has sex outside of heterosexual marriage, or steals from people before baptism, is not to give in to those habits ever again once he or she has made the conscious decision to lead the life of someone serving Christ. These convictions are shared among the members of all Protestant churches.

Depending on the denomination, an adherent could be baptized after several months of religious instruction by memorizing various verses from the Holy Bible. The Baptist faith and the Church of the Nazarene follow this approach in the initiation of church members. In other denominations, such as *Kor de Kri* (Body of Christ) Pentecostals, people who convert can become members the same day through full immersion baptism.[10] In Haiti church members receive an identification card that many bring with them when they migrate to the Bahamas. The card not only represents their membership in a Protestant church but also tangible evidence of eternal life in God's heavenly kingdom.

Membership in a Haitian Protestant church has its privileges. Members are allowed to participate in *lasentsen* (communion), the symbolic consumption of the blood and flesh of Jesus (wine and communion wafer). After baptism, members also participate in members meetings and pay their *dim* (tithes) required for membership. A research consultant who was denied membership at New Mission in New Providence for years because of *plasaj* (her common-law relationship) admitted that in order to participate in the choir, she decided to be baptized at her former church in Haiti. Singing in the choir was a privilege extended only to church members.

A church member, symbolically represented through the ornate church robes of the adult choir and participation in *lasentsen*, stands in contrast to the believer. Anthropologist Frederick Conway observes that it is important to understand that conversion to Protestantism does not necessarily mean becoming a member of a Protestant church organization. These *zanmi legliz* (friends of the church) take part in church activities but have not been baptized. Haitian believers—whether in the Bahamas, Haiti, or the United States—are necessary for churches to operate and maintain themselves. Churches rely on the offerings of believers. Whether they are part of the higher church hierarchy or have been baptized recently, members try to convince believers to become members in various ways. Through church sermons and testimony at *jènn* and witnessing, church members constantly try to assimilate believers. Church groups like *gwoup dom* (men's group) and *gwoup dam* (women's group) of Victory Chapel Church of the Nazarene set out to demonstrate that being a church member has its privileges. These privileges take on greater meaning when one is a migrant living apart from family and friends in the Bahamas where one is treated like a repugnant other. Again, the pastors and church members in New Providence whom I interviewed emphasized the importance of baptism as a clear path to salvation and eternal life in heaven.

When one visits a Haitian Protestant church in New Providence, one can easily tell members and believers apart by watching carefully during two events: the collection of offerings and *lasentsen* ceremonies. During the offering portion of *lekòl de Dimanch* (Sunday school) morning services, members place dues and tithes in special envelopes and baskets that the church passes out. Believers, by contrast, do not tithe; they pass up the special envelopes containing tithes and dues for the church and adult Sunday school and put their money on collection plates.

Lasentsen ceremonies, which are held on the first Sunday of every month, provide another occasion to observe the separation of believers from members. For example, as part of the *lasentsen* procedure at Victory Chapel Church of the Nazarene and at New Haitian Mission Baptist Church, members of the church rise from the pews to get their communion wine and wafer. While church members remain standing, believers sit because they are not allowed to participate in the ritual. At first glance, it seems that pastors make members stand and believers sit in order to put pressure on believers to become church members. It may have this effect on people.[11] Through *lasentsen*, believers are not only symbolically excluded from the church but from heaven as well because they have not been baptized. So *lasentsen*, as performed and orchestrated by the church hierarchy, can also be considered a mechanism that pastors and church members use in an attempt to convince believers to become members. After a Sunday church service at Prémière L'Église Baptiste de Port-au-Prince, Haiti, Rue de la Réunion in 2002, I, along with my cousins who were not baptized at the time, were made to stand outside of the church while my aunt stayed inside the church and participated in the *lasentsen* service.

Behavior and Appearance in Haitian Protestant Churches in New Providence

Sociologist and Haitian Protestantism expert Charles Poisset Romain (1986) has identified four Latin principles that characterize Protestantism in Haiti: Solus Christus (only Christ) with its corollaries, sola gratia (only Grace), sola fide (only Faith), and sola scriptura (only Scripture). All four principles form the basis of Soli Deo Gloria, or Glory only to God. Each of the churches I studied in New Providence exhibited all of these beliefs. In addition to their rejection of Vodou and their belief in tenets that are common to Haitian Protestantism, New Mission, Victory Chapel, and International Tabernacle of Praise interacted with each other and with the greater Haitian Protestant migrant community on a routine basis. There were times when the pastors and their respective congregants attended each other's churches and worshipped together. All three churches were represented at the weeklong International Crusade that took place in May 2005. Also, in a show of support, the pastors of New Mission and Victory Chapel preached at a two-week-long first anniversary celebration of International Tabernacle of Praise.[12] Sunday morning church services at all three churches were very similar in that all three had structured programs that followed a similar format each Sunday.[13]

Regardless of the denomination, baptized members of a Protestant church in Haiti are part of a religious culture that stresses certain forms of appearance and behavior for its community members. In Haiti, their asceticism made them distinct from Catholics and Vodou adherents and also demonstrated a commitment to their religious identity. This part of Protestantism in Haiti gives devout transmigrants a lens they look through and by which they can evaluate the state of their churches and, by extension, the state of their diasporic religious community. The difference between the way members and believers dressed and conducted themselves inside and outside the churches caused a good deal of social friction. This aspect of Haitian Protestant culture has come to the fore among Protestant churches in New Providence, Bahamas, which are described by migrants as *touloutoutou* and *tet mare* churches.

Touloutoutou and *Tet Mare* Churches

New Providence has at least two types of Haitian Protestant churches where we find the symbolic boundaries of *Kretyen, Pwotestan,* and *moun ki poko konvèti*. One type of church is sometimes called a *touloutoutou* (or *tilititi*) church and the other a *tet mare* church. *Touloutoutou* is an onomatopoeia that ridicules the sound and type of French spoken by the middle and upper classes of Haiti. *Tet mare* is a pejorative term that refers to the Haitian peasantry and is used by some Haitian Protestants to categorize churches where services are conducted primarily in Haitian Creole and adherents worship in an energetic fashion.

When adherents use these and other denigrating terms to describe the types of churches they do not like to attend, they do more than insult and stereotype practitioners of different types of Haitian Protestant Christianity. First, the use of these terms demarcates the use of French, the high prestige language in Haiti, from Haitian Creole, the low prestige language of Haiti, during church services. Second, the terms also reflect and replicate class tensions evident within Haitian society, tensions that some Haitians had attempted to escape through the act of migration.

Third, the use of these terms also reflects styles of religious practice each migrant considers to be "more Christian" than the other.

As part of a growing religious community, Haitian Protestants draw symbolic boundaries to develop a general sense of organization and order in New Providence. They use boundaries like *touloutoutou* and *tet mare* to reinforce collective norms and reinstate order within a social context outside of Haiti. Symbolic boundaries that reference language usage and social class have developed over time within Haitian Protestantism's two major religious traditions: historical (or puritanical) Protestantism and Pentecostal and charismatic Protestantism.[14] Historical Protestantism refers to the earlier forms of Protestant Christianity in Haiti that began when the Wesleyan Missionary Society established a missionary base in 1817. This includes the Methodist and Baptist faiths and stresses reserved, sober, and unemotional forms of worship and an austere dress code for its adherents. Pentecostal and charismatic Protestantism grew exponentially during François Duvalier's reign (1957–1971) as he sought to weaken the powers of the Catholic Church. Haiti was flooded with American missionaries who provided the Haitian populace with social services that the state was responsible for, such as education and potable water. Pentecostal and charismatic forms of Christianity stress energetic worship that is guided by *lasentespri* (the Holy Spirit). In interviews, migrants referred to historical Protestant churches as *touloutoutou* churches, or as churches that were *Batis* (Baptist) and *twò Batis* (very Baptist). Members and believers of these traditional Protestant churches sometimes referred to adherents of Pentecostal and charismatic churches as *les trembleurs*, the French term for tremblers.

In her research among white male members of the French and American upper-middle classes, sociologist Michèle Lamont uses the concept of symbolic boundaries to analyze what it means to be a worthy person among elites. Symbolic boundaries, she notes, are "conceptual distinctions that [humans] make to categorize objects, people, practices, and even time and space" (Lamont 1992, 9). Through boundary work we construct ourselves and define who we are. With symbolic boundaries we also both abstractly and concretely define people with whom we do not

want to associate, people to whom we consider ourselves to be superior
or inferior, and people who arouse hostility, indifference and sympa-
thy within us (xvii). Along these lines Lamont contends that a significant portion of our daily activities are oriented toward avoiding shame
and maintaining a positive self-identity by patrolling the borders of the
groups to which we belong (11). At a macrosociological level, this boundary work is used to reinstate order within communities by reinforcing
collective norms, as boundaries provide a way to develop a general sense
of organization and order in the environment (11).

Sister Edwidge and Touloutoutou *Churches*

Although French is the high prestige language in Haiti, the majority
Creole-speaking populace ridicules French speakers with pejoratives
like *touloutoutou*. The implicit meaning of *touloutoutou* conveys issues
of superiority and is emblematic of Haiti's elites and bourgeois classes
who speak French. Reflections from a devout Haitian Protestant woman
named Sister Edwidge, who attended services at International Tabernacle
of Praise, illuminate the use of this term.

When I approached her for an interview, I falsely assumed that Sister
Edwidge was a member of the church and lived in the Bahamas. She
lived in Port-au-Prince, Haiti, and came to the Bahamas only a few times
a year on business. She is a *komèsan*, a job that many Haitian women
throughout the region hold. A *komèsan* buys and sells goods at markets
and among her neighbors. Edwidge learned the trade from her mother
and traveled to the Bahamas, the Dominican Republic, Haiti, Panama,
and the United States to buy and sell goods. During the interview Sister
Edwidge revealed that her family practiced Vodou. When she was growing up in Verrettes, located in the Artibonite department of Haiti, Sister
Edwidge's mother would take her often to Vodou ceremonies. But at the
age of twenty-six, she converted to Pentecostalism as the result of a series
of events that highlight one reason that Haitians convert to Protestant
forms of Christianity: as a way to manage illnesses (Métraux 1959).

A pain developed in her waist and foot and persisted for days, so Sister Edwidge's family brought her to a Vodou priest for a medical consultation. A shared belief among many Haitians is that causes of illness are spiritual and can be addressed through religion. Often such consultations are with an *oungan* (Vodou priest) or *manbo* (Vodou priestess) who employs *maji* to discern which *lwa* (ancestral spirit) is causing the malady in order to placate that *lwa* in an effort to arrive at a cure. This did not work for Sister Edwidge. Then, while asleep one night, she heard a voice tell her that if she did not convert (to a Protestant denomination) she would die. When she awoke the next morning, she told family members what had occurred in the middle of the night. They told her that if the same thing had happened to them, they would convert. She waited a week before she decided to. Sister Edwidge imparted her revelation to a close friend, who then took her to a Pentecostal church on the following Sunday where the pastors prayed with her. At that moment she was set on the path to become Sister Edwidge, a disciple of Jesus Christ. The malady that caused Sister Edwidge so much anguish went away and, as of 2005, had not recurred. She explained the type of Haitian Protestant church and style of worship she is careful to avoid in the Bahamas while there on business:

> Sometimes Haitian Baptists do not say, "Hallelujah!" They don't say, "Hallelujah!" "Glory to God!" . . . And they sing *solanelman* [in a solemn, reserved fashion;[15] at this point, Sister Edwidge imitates how Baptists sing at a *touloutoutou* church, starting with the beginning of the first verse of the second selection from the French section of Chants d'espérance]:
> "*Grand Dieu nous te bénissons, Nous célébrons . . .*"
> You understand? And Pentecostals sing. . . . [Sister Edwidge now sings at a faster pace while clapping her hands]: "*Alelouya, glwa a Dye! Alelouya!* (Hallelujah, glory to God! Hallelujah!)" There's a difference.[16]

As Sister Edwidge described how worshipping in a Pentecostal manner filled her with the Holy Spirit and the joy of God, she also explained some of the key features of *touloutoutou* churches. First, she was relieved that Haitian Baptist churches in the Bahamas were more charismatic in nature than the Baptist churches she was accustomed to in Port-au-Prince, Haiti, where the musical style employed in the worship and praise portion of services is deliberate and reserved, reflecting the manner and strict behavior representative at *touloutoutou* churches (a member of a Pentecostal or charismatic church would describe this style as *fret* [cold]).[17]

Sister Edwidge continued her comparison of Baptist traditions to her Pentecostal tradition by outlining other differences between the two kinds of worshippers:

Baptists, I don't know but this is me saying this, they don't really believe in the Holy Spirit and they don't think a person can be touched by the Holy Spirit, but Pentecostals don't have a problem because you're worshipping God and you feel something that is in you that gives you a push. You say hallelujah very loud! But if you go to a Baptist church and do that in Haiti, [the church goes] after you. [But when you do this] in a Baptist church . . . in the Bahamas? They're not shocked by it. They don't have a problem with that.

They only speak French [at Baptist churches in Haiti] . . . and if you go to church and scream, "Hallelujah," the pastor says, "Put him/her outside for me," because that person is *sòt* [stupid]. S/He is going to disrupt things and excite the *fidel* [faithful ones]. But if you go to Pastor Jean-Marie's church [the head pastor of a large Pentecostal church in Port-au-Prince, Haiti at the time of our interview], you say, "Hallelujah" [she screams again]. Then everyone is happy and sees the Holy Spirit in their midst.

It's there where I get that feeling. Because God has a thing hidden inside of Him. If you make your body small, you'll find it inside [of your body]. And that's why I love God. I decided to stay and serve the Lord until the very end. Because I see it's something that you're not even thinking about. A thing maybe that's not even in my spirit in the moment or you have sadness in your heart or you're thinking of a thing that hurts you.

And then in that moment, you feel a song come to your mouth, and then you feel a push to say, "Hallelujah!" And then in the same place you feel that your heart has changed, you feel that your mouth has changed. You come to have another experience. A person can't stop me from believing this.[18]

As Sister Edwidge observes, services at *touloutoutou* churches are held in French, the language of the Haitian elite. The hymns sung at the Sunday morning service, for instance, are mostly from the French section of Chants d'espérance (a Baptist hymnal called "Songs of Hope"). The pastor's sermon is delivered in French and the Bible used, *La Sainte Bible* (the Holy Bible), is written in French.

The emotional restraint of congregants at *touloutoutou* churches is another key feature that truly distinguishes them from Pentecostal and charismatic churches. At the First Baptist Church of Port-au-Prince calling out "Hallelujah," "Amen," and "Glory to God" are considered unacceptable emotional outbursts. However, believers and members of Pentecostal and charismatic churches view these so-called outbursts differently. Emotional expressions such as these are interpreted as the power of the Holy Spirit manifesting itself in a congregant. At a *touloutoutou* church, the head pastor, an evangelist, or a pastor from a visiting church are the only people allowed to raise their voices and the congregation can respond with a reserved amen when appropriate.[19] In the event that someone sitting in the pews of a *touloutoutou* church does call out "Hallelujah" during a service, that person would most likely be removed from the church and would be considered disruptive. While *touloutoutou* churches are regarded as prestigious, this type of church reifies class divisions in Haitian society by elevating congregants to a higher category than Protestants who practice Pentecostal and charismatic forms of Protestantism in Haiti.

Ultimately, Sister Edwidge and other migrants, including pastors and church members, described the emotionally restrained worship at historical Protestant churches in Haiti as representative of a religious style that was behind the times. Later in her interview, she categorized churches where congregants are not allowed to let the Holy Spirit manifest itself as *an reta* (late). The implication of her comments is that Pentecostal or charismatic style of worship, found at *tet mare* churches, is spiritually liberating, more advanced, and more Christian than the style of worship found at *touloutoutou* churches because Pentecostal and charismatic forms of Protestant Christianity invite the Holy Spirit in their midst and allow people to express themselves without restraint. In other words, traditional Haitian Baptist churches, in Sister Edwidge's opinion, are shackled by traditions that prevent true religious expression and proximity to God. Sister Edwidge's critique of *touloutoutou* churches inverts the existing socio-religious order where puritanical Protestants are at the top and Pentecostal and charismatic Protestants are at the bottom. This is also a reflection of their social class standing.

Although the style of worship at *touloutoutou* churches is more restrained and dour, the physical appearance and behavior of Pentecostal and charismatic Haitian Protestants is arguably stricter than the behavioral standards found in *touloutoutou* churches. Those behavioral standards reflect a moral discipline that *tet mare* adherents believe is lacking at historical Protestant churches in Haiti. Pentecostal and charismatic women, for example, are supposed to be plain in appearance and dress, and tend not to wear any makeup, in contrast to women from historical Haitian Protestant traditions who wear wigs and makeup. The appearance of both groups of adherents, however, is collectively stricter than Haitian Catholics and Vodou practitioners and *Kretyen* adherents can be found in both types of churches in New Providence.

Brother Bicha *and* Boujou Goujou Goujou *Churches*

Most Haitian Protestant churches in New Providence lean toward charismatic forms of worship during services. However, not all of the members of the religious community choose to worship and praise God in that fashion. Brother Bicha prefers the type of worship and praise practiced at traditional or puritanical Haitian Protestant churches. Born and raised on La Tortue, Haiti's most northern island, Brother Bicha, like many of my informants from *depatman Nòdwès* (the Northwestern department of Haiti), grew up with parents who were not married and family members who used Vodou as a way to deal with illness and misfortune. As an adolescent he became interested in the Bible and began to question the religious teachings he had received at the Episcopal and Catholic schools he attended in his youth. He accepted Christ in the early 1990s through a friend in La Tortue who prayed with him.

In 1998 he could not find any type of employment in Haiti so he migrated to the Bahamas. After his arrival in New Providence, he visited Calvary Baptist Church, New Haitian Mission Baptist Church, Victory Chapel, and Emmäus, the oldest Haitian Baptist church in New Providence. Brother Bicha decided that he should attend Calvary, where he was baptized in 2001. My research consultants identified Calvary as the only Baptist church in the community at that time that worshipped in a manner closest to the type of traditional Baptist church found in Haiti (a *touloutoutou* Protestant church).

Brother Bicha considered himself to be part of Haiti's middle-class. His mother was a *komèsan* and his father was a carpenter and mason. Brother Bicha recalled managing money prudently at a young age, a skill that would serve him well in his adult life. Upon my initial arrival at his apartment, I was struck by how different it was from the squalid living spaces that many Haitians in New Providence occupied. I had interviewed Sister Edwidge on a porch in an alley where people passed by and garbage was strewn about. By contrast, Brother Bicha and his wife lived in a two-bedroom apartment that contained newer furniture and reflected his middle-class aspirations. Pictures of their wedding, for example, were carefully displayed in their living room, which also included plants, an armoire, loveseat, chair, and sofa. His residence stood in stark contrast to the majority of apartments and homes in which I conducted my interviews and which were overcrowded, poorly furnished, and often infested with cockroaches and rats.

Brother Bicha discussed his life in great detail, switching between French and English at the beginning, and then articulating the rest of his thoughts in a mélange of Haitian Creole and English. Some of his future plans included becoming a businessman and completing the construction of a house in Haiti. He described his initial search for a church in which he could *"santi prezans Bondyè* [feel the presence of God]":

> The first church I visited was Calvary Baptist Church. I visited Calvary because of my brother. He was already there. It was his church, where he was. And then the longer he went to church there, [my brother stayed there]. He brought me there. Then after that, I visited some other churches. . . . I visited Pastor Exanté's church [New Haitian Mission Baptist Church]. . . . I just visited a few times. . . . The reason why I didn't stay there . . . I didn't . . . I didn't feel comfortable with their doctrine, the way they taught. . . . When [I visited] New Mission, it resembled a Pentecostal church, the way they worshipped, because . . . [of] the way they worship. . . . After that I went to Pastor Antoine's church [Victory Chapel].
>
> The church I left in Haiti had a UEBH [Union of Evangelical Baptists in Haiti][20] doctrine and they . . . were really *annòd* [in order]. They didn't have a bunch of loud *"boujou goujou goujou"* music!
>
> My church in Haiti had cymbals and tambourines. When they would sing with the music, the music was played low, very low. And then it wasn't too "hot" like Pentecostal churches. And it wasn't the law of the church for you to dance "sweet" inside of the church. Biblically, you don't dance a lot like that in church. Whereas, when I visited Calvary sometimes, I can compare it with my church that I left in Haiti, Ebenezer. Because I saw that [Calvary Baptist Church was similar to Ebenezer]. Calvary did their services in French and Creole. Also the people at my church in Haiti clapped their hands in a way that was disciplined. When you clap your hands you can't [wildly] clap your hands; when I'm sitting next to you and you're [really] clapping your hands . . . you're almost hitting me. We [at Calvary] clap our hands *nan lòd* (in an orderly way), in a common way.[21]

Brother Bicha's comments concerning New Haitian Mission Baptist Church revealed his aversion to Pentecostal and charismatic-style worship. During my five months at New Mission the deacon, a former Nazarene church member, led prayers and hymns that energized the congregation in anticipation of the sermons of Dr. Exanté or a visiting *predikatè* (preacher; deliverer of the word of God). The deacon's orchestration of the worship and praise portion of Sunday morning services was similar to the manner and style of service that the assistant pastor conducted at Victory Chapel Church of the Nazarene, which is the other church Brother Bicha visited and disliked because of its charismatic worship style. His diaspora church contained similar features of *touloutoutou* churches. His former church in Haiti resembled a style found in the First Baptist Church of Port-au-Prince, a *touloutoutou* church that is part of the Union of Evangelical Baptists in Haiti (UEBH), a fellowship of Baptist churches established in 1928.

Brother Bicha's *"boujou goujou goujou"* comment reflects another onomatopoeia that symbolizes noise and serves as a disparaging reference to the volume and style of musical worship found at Pentecostal and charismatic churches. In his interviews with Haitian Pentecostals in Haiti and in Brooklyn, New York, ethnomusicologist Melvin Butler found that most of his research consultants expressed a preference for music that is *cho* (hot), as opposed to the *fret* (cold) styles traditionally favored by Adventist and Baptist Haitians. In both independent and organizational churches, *cho* styles of Pentecostal musical worship feature lively tempos, energetic use of the body, highly emotional singing, and constant, driving rhythmic accompaniment, all of which are geared toward evoking the felt presence of the Holy Spirit (Butler 2002, 95).

But the "hot" style of musical worship, the "sweet" dancing between the aisles and the pews of church, and the "chaotic" hand clapping are what Brother Bicha found undesirable in his view of proper Protestant Christian worship. The use of the terms *lòd* (an orderly way) and *annòd* (in order) in his explanation of worship at his churches in Haiti and the Bahamas represent his belief in so-called respectable and appropriate worship in church. His concern with order also reflects a type of comportment that is part of a religious habitus he developed starting at Ebenezer, his church in Haiti, and continued at Calvary Baptist Church in New Providence. Brother Bicha's aspirations as a businessman and a Christian require that he manifest a comportment that is similar to other adherents at Calvary Baptist Church. Although the behavioral standards at *tet mare* churches are stricter, they manifest what anthropologist Diane Austin-Broos (1997, 9) calls in her study of Jamaican Pentecostalism "eudemonic rite," the joyful celebration of healing rite, accompanied by lively music and expressive dance, precisely the kinds of religious behavior that Brother Bicha regards as obstacles on his path to a bourgeois existence.

Tet mare churches are increasingly popular in Haiti and in the Bahamas because they legitimize enthusiasm and spirit possession; both are aspects of widespread Haitian religious practice, specifically Vodou. Haitian ruling classes have long denigrated Vodou because of its African origins. The growth of *tet mare* Protestant Christianity in Haitian religion is in part explicable by the freedom of emotional expression that this form of religious practice invites and encourages, placing one in direct contact with the Holy Spirit, the ultimate leveler of human distinctions. Consequently, this freedom of expression renders *tet mare* a "truer" form of Christianity from the standpoint of its adherents, than what is practiced in *touloutoutou* churches.

In effect, *touloutoutou* and *tet mare* churches are mutually exclusive religious spaces. Members of each generally denigrate members of the other. When *touloutoutou*, *tet mare*, and other religious boundaries are invoked by Haitian Protestants in the Bahamas, they also reflect social class differences and intrareligious tensions that demonstrate a struggle among Haitian Protestants to define which type of Protestant Christianity is authentic, that is, which is more Christian and thus morally and materially superior.

There are numerous factors that unite and divide Haitian Protestants. A shared vocabulary and a rejection of Vodou, Haiti's folk religion, are common to devout Haitian Protestants in a transnational social field. A Protestant ethic allows Haitian Protestant migrants to accumulate capital that is used to sustain family abroad and fund future migration to another destination in the North American region. Devout Haitian Protestant migrants also pay close attention to the behavior and appearance of members of their religious communities as a way to gauge whether or not people are maturing in their respective faiths.

Behavior and appearance, though, can become divisive factors among Haitian Protestants who practice puritanical forms of Haitian Protestantism like the Adventist and Baptist faiths and charismatic forms of Haitian Protestantism like Pentecostalism (Corten 2001). *Touloutoutou* and *tet mare* not only reflect symbolic boundaries but also illustrate a tension within the community of Haitian Protestants in New Providence, reflecting the reality of class tensions in Haiti and the Haitian diaspora.

Chapter 2 offers a look at the lives of Haitians in the Bahamas. Haitians are the largest immigrant group in the Bahamas and are viewed as a threat to the nation's sovereignty and social stability if their migration continues unabated. Yet, as we will see, an alternative view of the Haitian diaspora emphasizes the ways in which Bahamian society creates a permanent Haitian underclass that partly facilitates Bahamian prosperity. Using historical analysis and ethnographic research, the chapter demonstrates how the Bahamian state exploits Haitian labor, how contemporary Bahamian identity relies on the construction of a repugnant Haitian "other," and how Bahamians of Haitian descent, referred to popularly as "Haitian-Bahamians," are rendered stateless by Bahamian law. The result is that the Bahamas has become a liminal space where Haitians are marginalized and Haitian identity is highly stigmatized, leading Haitian Protestant migrants to draw on their religiosity as a key resource in their attempts to live a dignified life.

2

Haitians in the Bahamas

While in New Providence, I accepted an invitation to speak to children about the importance of education in their lives.[1] I met with them at an after-school program in one of the poorer neighborhoods. The children, who sat around me in a circle and ranged in age from five to ten, were black and of primarily African descent. I spoke to them about my educational development in the United States and encouraged them to do well in their studies. I then sat down at a table with a few girls of grade-school age. During my stay-in-school speech, I noticed that one of the girls at the table was struck with a look of astonishment when I mentioned that I was of Haitian descent.

I took the opportunity to ask the girl why she looked so surprised when I mentioned my Haitian heritage. She replied that I did not look Haitian but Bahamian to her. I then asked her, "What does a Haitian look like?" She, and her fellow after-schoolmates, replied in Bahamian English: "They scrubby," which means that Haitians have "an uneven or mottled dark complexion" (Holm and Shilling 1982, 178). They also said of Haitians that "they black," "they smell bad," and "they look like rat."[2]

While it may surprise some that black Bahamian children would project a form of blackness onto Haitians that is loaded with undesirable and negative connotations, stereotypes that depict Haitians as an offensive "other" are common in the Bahamas. For example, Haitians may be considered a burden or strain on the country, using health care, education, and social services at the expense and exclusion of Bahamians, and as having a proclivity for violence (Fielding et al. 2008, 39).

These stereotypes are more than just insults. They reveal the invisible architecture of Bahamian society. As media studies professor Charles Ramírez Berg (1997, 116) has written in reference to stereotyping Hispanics in films: "The object of the game is not simply spotting stereotypes, but analyzing the system that endorses them. Once minority representations are seen and understood for what they are, the invisible architecture of the dominant-dominated 'arrangement' is exposed and there is a chance for a structural 'rearrangement.'" Stereotypes about Haitians in the Bahamas reflect how Bahamian society is structured for the benefit of Bahamians and through the exclusion of Haitians and those who can be legally defined as non-Bahamians. The stereotypes expressed by the children also reflect the marginality of Haitian life in the Bahamas. To help put my discussion in context, I begin with a description of Bay Street—a major thoroughfare in New Providence and one of the main tourist destinations in the country—as seen through the eyes of a tourist.

A Walk along Bay Street

Bay Street is a one-way street that heads east and cuts through downtown Nassau, the capital of the Bahamas. Along this bustling boulevard you see the Atlantic Ocean, beaches with crystal clear Bahamian water, and ocean liners carrying tourists from all over the world. On Bay Street, for a small fee, you can catch a ferry off of Prince Georges Wharf to Paradise Island. Paradise Island has million-dollar homes where Oprah Winfrey and Arnold Schwarzenegger are rumored to own properties and where the Atlantis hotel attracts visitors from all over the globe with its casino, world-famous aquarium, and water park. On small boats that seat anywhere from twenty to thirty people, tour guides recount a brief history of the Bahamas. The guides also provide useful demographic information about the Caribbean nation. They note that the archipelagic nation of the Bahamas is made up of seven hundred islands and cays, that it became an independent nation in 1973 through a peaceful transfer of power from a former colonial government, and that the island of New Providence,

New Providence, the Bahamas. Courtesy of Ermitte St. Jacques.

where two-thirds of the population of the country lives, runs twenty-one miles wide and seven miles long.

On your fifteen minute boat trip to Paradise Island your tour guide, who speaks English, the official language of the Bahamas, explains that the Bahamas is a commonwealth realm, one of sixteen sovereign states of the Commonwealth of Nations that separately recognize Queen Eliza-beth II as their monarch. At this moment the guide will note that the Bahamian economy is primarily dependent on "you guys," meaning tourists, and offshore banking. Tourism is the major economic strat-egy of modernization for the Bahamian state (Alexander 1997, 67). The tour guide may also mention that tourism accounts for 60 percent of the nation's gross domestic product and employs half of the labor force that makes the per capita income in the Bahamas the highest in the Caribbean and Latin America.

If you decide not to take the ferry to Paradise Island, you can con-tinue to walk east along Bay Street, where you can catch a glimpse of everyday life in New Providence. Bay Street is the spot where you can catch a bus to almost anywhere on the island, watching Bahamians on their way to work. It looks like many Bahamians are black. Indeed, most of the country is of African descent (85 percent), but until as recently as 1973, the country's small white minority dominated the political and social institutions of the country (Collinwood 1989, 27). Along Bay Street, you see Bahamians driving jitneys, compact buses that seat up to twenty people, taking the island's inhabitants where they need to go.

Many of the island's occupants are on their way to work at the hotels and resorts along Cable Beach, or to Arawak Cay (known to residents as the Fish Fry), where people eat seafood dishes of cracked conch, conch fritters, conch salad, and fried grouper at colorfully painted restaurants. Depending on the time of day, the buses are filled with children in uniforms who are on their way to school, home, or Marathon Mall, a popular hangout. On Sundays, many Bahamians use buses to get to church. The Bahamas prides itself for being a Christian nation where the majority of the inhabitants practice Catholic and Protestant forms of Christianity. Church is arguably more important to the Bahamian social fabric than school, government or, often, even the family. As sociologist Dean Collinwood reflects, the reason that church and religion are more important to the Bahamian social fabric is that the most important features of Bahamian life—conscience development, mate selection and marriage, and vital social activities—take place within the confines of the church (Collinwood 1989, 16).[3]

Continuing your walk east along Bay Street, you see banks and cruise ships docked on your left and pink buildings over your right shoulder. All government buildings are painted pink and public schools are painted yellow. A statue of Queen Victoria stands in a courtyard where the House of Assembly and the Senate are located. Off to the left is a large board featuring a crest with a swordfish, a flamingo, a conch shell, and one of the ships on which Columbus's expedition to the "New World" sailed. Below the crest it reads: "Forward, Upward, Onward Together." Based on this motto, the average visitor to the Bahamas would be correct in assuming that this archipelagic nation is a democratic society. This view is in line with other general views of the Bahamas as "paradise," generated by the brochures and commercials that attract tourists to the Bahamas

A Bahamian restaurant at Arawak Cay, June 2012.

(Strachan 2002, 1). But the same visitor would be wrong in assuming that he or she could easily become a citizen of the Bahamas or that the Bahamas is an inclusive society that embraces other nationalities. A look at the history of the Bahamas reveals why this nation is structured the way it is.

The Bahamas—A Brief History

The earliest inhabitants of what is now known as the Bahamas were the Lucayan Indians, who lived there from 500 to 1525 ce (Craton and Saunders 1992, 3). When Columbus encountered them in his travels to the Caribbean in the late fifteenth century, the Lucayans were brought against their will to the island of Hispaniola and then were decimated by deportation, disease, emigration, and outmarriage. The Bahamas were then virtually unoccupied until settlers from Bermuda and England arrived between 1644 and 1647. In 1718 it became a British colony and in the late 1700s the population increased from the influx of approximately

"Forward, Upward, Onward Together" placard, June 2012.

eight thousand Loyalists and their enslaved Africans, who moved to the Bahamas from New York, Florida, and the Carolinas.

As historian Howard Johnson (1991) observes, the colonial experience in the Bahamas was atypical in comparison to the rest of the West Indies in that the Bahamian colonial economy tended to be commercial and extractive in nature rather than based on the export of major agricultural staples common to the Caribbean such as coffee, indigo, sugar, and tobacco. According to Johnson, the Bahamas utilized a task and self-hire system during slavery and the evolution and operation of long-term labor contracts were introduced in connection with the liberated Africans who were settled in the Bahamas (Johnson 1991, vii). Starting after Emancipation in 1838, the predominantly black labor force was effectively controlled by a white agro-commercial and mercantile minority. This white minority would maintain their hegemony in the Bahamas for another 129 years. Though Blacks were no longer enslaved, they were effectively barred from important roles in the English colonial administration and from lucrative economic pursuits. Blacks were also denied full citizenship rights and were exploited by the white autocracy (Collinwood 1989, 27).

From 1880 to 1920, there was large-scale migration within the Caribbean, driven by depressed economic conditions in most of the Caribbean territories and by a demand for labor in certain countries in the Caribbean and Central America where European and American interests expanded capital investments (Johnson 1991, 149). Skilled West Indian laborers went to the Bahamas to work starting in 1922 with the rebuilding of the Colonial Hotel. Work opportunities for skilled West Indian immigrants in the Bahamas continued until 1926. During that time the Grove and the Cable Beach areas of New Providence were developed for wealthy Americans who spent their winters there (Johnson 1991, 151). Around 1926 measures were taken by the Bahamian government to restrict the flow of West Indian immigrants due to a decrease in opportunities in the labor market.

Tourism soon became the backbone of the Bahamian economy. Between World War I and World War II, tourism grew internationally. Much of the success of the tourist industry in the Bahamas was a result of the upswing in the economy during the Prohibition era in the United States. According to historian Gail Saunders (2000, 73), Nassau, a transshipment port for smuggling liquor into the United States, benefited greatly from rum-running profits. Those profits led to the improvement of the infrastructure of New Providence. As the tourism of elites from the 1920s and 1930s gave way to the mass tourism of the 1950s, 1960s, and 1970s,[4] deleterious social effects coincided with economic benefits. The influx of American tourists and real estate developers inflated the cost of living and made it difficult for the majority of the laboring class and migrants from the Out Islands (the other islands that make up the Bahamas with the exception of New Providence and Grand Bahama) to earn a living. They were forced to migrate to New Providence because of the neglect of the Out Islands (78).[5] Although tourism allowed for the upward mobility of a large percentage of the Bahamian population, it also damaged Bahamian ecosystems, widened the gap between the rich (mostly white) and poor (mostly black), and exacerbated existing racial tensions.

While a small part of the new wealth from tourism trickled down to the black majority, who worked in the tourist industry and were generally gracious and friendly hosts for foreign visitors, it was not enough to move the majority of Bahamians into the middle-class (Collinwood 1989, 28). In 1953, eleven years after a riot broke out between Bahamian and American laborers, the Progressive Liberal Party (PLP) was formed with the goal of gaining power for the country's black majority. In early 1958 a general strike occurred due to an agreement that Nassau hotel operators made with a tour company and a white-owned taxicab company to transport people between the new airport and the hotels of Nassau. This agreement would have deprived black cab drivers of a very lucrative portion of their business. The strike shut down the tourist industry, which severely affected the Bahamian economy, and black taxi drivers won the right to drive passengers from the airport. As a result of the display of black economic power demonstrated by the strike, the government of Great Britain added four more seats to the Bahamian house of Assembly that were all won by the black-majority PLP in elections in 1960 (28).

When the government refused to accept amendments to the bill by which the electoral boundaries were to be redrawn on April 27, 1965, Lynden O. Pindling, the leader of the PLP, threw the mace, the symbol of the Speaker's authority, out of the window of the House of Assembly and into the street packed with demonstrators. This symbolic act galvanized the black majority and struck fear into the hearts of the white merchants and lawyers who controlled Bahamian politics known as the Bay Street Boys. By 1967 the PLP had won control of the government and then the Bahamas became an independent member of the British Commonwealth of Nations in 1973 (28–29).

Since independence the PLP has built upon the inherited tourism economy. The Bahamian economy was successful in that the standard of living of many Bahamians improved significantly. But some of the challenges Bahamians face stem not only from the downside of tourism but also from the growth of its Haitian migrant population and how the Bahamian state deals with immigration. The Bahamian state tries to control the Haitian population through immigration laws, work permit programs, and the repatriation of undocumented migrants.

Haitian Migration to the Bahamas

Haitians migrate from Haiti to other parts of the Caribbean (Dominica, Jamaica, Guadeloupe and Martinique) and North America during times of economic uncertainty, political repression, and social unrest. Although Haitians have been part of the wave of recent immigration to the United States in the twentieth and twenty-first centuries, the Haitian presence in the United States is not a recent migratory phenomenon but part of a larger trend that dates back to the eighteenth century. We can view this history as a stream with high, low, and dormant periods (Laguerre

1998, 2). Similarly, Haitian migration to the Bahamas is not a recent phenomenon but the continuation of a larger trend. The first large influx of Haitians to the Bahamas occurred around the time of the Haitian revolution (1791–1803). As enslaved Africans fought against white planters, migrants primarily from the bourgeoisie, French colonists, their slaves, and some free blacks fled Haiti (Treco 2002, 3). The intended destinations for most of these migrants were Cuba or the United States, but as historian Michael Craton (1995) has noted, many ended up either in Jamaica or the Bahamas. It was this group of migrants that accounts for the prevalence of French surnames among modern Bahamians: Bodie, Delevaux, Deveaux, Duvalier, Moncur, Poitier, and Symonette. These names reveal how many modern Bahamians can trace part of their creolized heritage to Haiti.

By December 1957 the Bahamian Immigration Department estimated the number of Haitians in the colony to be nearly one thousand (Marshall 1979, 99). The second large influx of Haitians to the Bahamas was during the time of the Duvalier dictatorship in Haiti that lasted from 1957 to 1986 under François "Papa Doc" Duvalier (1957–1971) and Jean-Claude "Baby Doc" Duvalier (1971–1986). The use of extreme violence by Papa Doc to maintain his regime forced many Haitians to flee their country. Between 1957 and 1962 Haitian migration to the Bahamas increased to approximately ten thousand, comprising almost 15 percent of the total population of the Bahamas (Tinker 2011, 105). By 1969 approximately twenty thousand Haitians had migrated to the Bahamas, with the majority from the lower classes of Haiti's poorest regions (Treco 2002, 3).

The third major influx of Haitians to the Bahamas started in 1985 as pressure mounted in Haiti for the end to the Duvalier regime (Treco 2002). When President-for-Life Jean-Claude left aboard an American chartered jet in 1986, migration from Haiti continued unabated due to continued poverty, unemployment, and political instability. Neoliberalism—a set of economic and development policies characterized by privatization, marketization, and an unregulated "free" market—was an external factor that also encouraged out-migration from Haiti (Waterston

2006, 135). These guidelines, followed by other exploited countries in Africa, the Caribbean, and Latin America, exacerbated the already difficult socioeconomic conditions of the poor in their respective countries. Fostering an export-oriented economy, lowering wages to attract foreign investment, and reducing social spending to guarantee debt repayment further deteriorated the standard of living of the poor majority of Haitians (St. Jacques 2001, 25). "By the end of the twentieth century Haiti's combination of an economic system based on the exploitation of peasant farmers and the enrichment of a privileged minority, and a predatory state making negligible investments in human resources and basic infrastructure, had created a socio-economic crisis of staggering proportions" (Arthur and Dash 1999, 111). These factors, along with the kleptocratic Duvalier regimes, contributed to Haiti's status as the poorest country in the Western Hemisphere, and one of the twenty-five poorest countries in the world.[6]

Haitians do not necessarily migrate to the Bahamas with the intention of settling there (Craton 1995; Craton and Saunders 1998; Marshall 1979). Many Haitians travel to the Bahamas with the intention of living and working there temporarily to support their families abroad, and an overall goal of improving their future lives in Haiti. For example, Brother Bicha, who attended Calvary Baptist Church and had lived in the Bahamas for over six years at the time of our interview in 2005, returned to Haiti periodically to visit relatives, build a home, and planned to start a business there once conditions improved.

Many of my research consultants mentioned that Haitians migrate there as a stepping-stone to future migration to the United States. Great Inagua, the island furthest south in the Bahamian archipelago, is fifty-five miles from La Tortue, an island that forms the northern most part of Haiti's Northwestern department. These "flow-through" migrants use boats as a form of transportation, journey to the Bahamas, and work to make money to repay those who funded their initial passage, as well as plan for future migration to the United States. Anthropologist Ermitte St. Jacques (2001, 7) observes that the migration of Haitians to the Bahamas has a "stair/step" quality to it in that the poorest nations send migrants to the less poor countries, and the less poor countries send migrants to industrialized nations.

Bahamian Laws and the Formation of a Haitian Underclass

Most Haitians find their way to the island of New Providence by boat and plane. Whether in the Bahamas temporarily or for longer periods of time, Haitians usually do the jobs that Bahamians do not do. Bahamians depend on Haitians for agricultural and gardening labor. Haitian men also clean hotels, and work as carpenters, construction workers, and landscapers. Other Haitian men in New Providence cook and bus tables at restaurants, and serve as electricians, handymen, painters, mechanics, and tailors. Haitian women work at restaurants, braid hair, sell goods, and serve as cashiers at duty-free liquor stores and gas stations.

Employment for Haitians in the Bahamas is governed by the work permit program, which is described by the Yale Human Rights Delegation Report on Haitians in the Bahamas as resembling "indentured servitude." The system requires that a Haitian find a Bahamian employer, who will apply for the required permit on the Haitian's behalf to the authorities. The permit bears the employer's name, and Haitian employees are left with no flexibility to change jobs or to seek other employment if they fall out of the good graces of the employer. Workers usually bear the cost of their permits, often over time, on credit to the employer (Yale Human Rights Delegation Report 1994).

According to the Yale report, the Bahamian government doubled the price of permits in May 1993: permits for domestics rose from $250 to $500, for tailors from $1,000 to $2,000, and for farm workers from $25 to $250. These sums often amount to more than a month's wages for Haitians. The increases have an exclusionary effect, adding to the number of Haitians who work without proper documentation, and they increase their vulnerability to and dependence on the whims of their employers. The increased costs of permits are also paired with a requirement that workers pay retroactive national insurance premiums, amounts that can run into hundreds of dollars, adding to the general climate of oppression according to the Yale report. The system is supported by the threat of detention and repatriation if a Haitian either does not repay the costs of the work permit and the insurance or is caught working without proper documentation. It is no wonder, then, that black Bahamians casually refer to black Haitians they employ as "my Haitian," a term that evokes a master-slave relationship.

In addition to laws that safeguard employment opportunities for Bahamians, the Bahamian government has used a strategy of strengthening existing immigration laws and repatriating undocumented migrants throughout the mid-twentieth century to the present. Both strategies serve as ways to control the entry of Haitians into the Bahamas. The Bahamian authorities have been concerned about Haitian migration since 1957. At times the Bahamian government has intensified its efforts to control the Haitian migrant population through raids (known as *round-ups*), internment in detention centers, and, in 1963 and 1967, deportation (Marshall 1979). In 1963 the Bahamian Immigration Department began "Operation Clean Up," which was designed to repatriate an estimated ten thousand undocumented Haitians who were working and living in the Bahamas (see Tinker 2011, 105).[7]

Additionally, a new Immigration Act was introduced in 1963 under a revised Constitution to target Haitian immigration. The new act replaced the Immigration Act of 1928, which had defined a Bahamian as a native of the colony, and "redefined the conditions under which a person could claim Bahamian citizenship, or 'belonger' status" (106). According to historian Keith Tinker (2011, 106) the Immigration Act of 1963 also granted immigration officers new powers to stem the tide of Haitian migration to the Bahamas such as searching people without a warrant, interrogating prospective immigrants, requesting medical certification, arresting people in cases of reasonable suspicion, and demanding letters of intent from non-Bahamians whenever they were requested. A "Vessels Restriction Regulations" also accompanied the new act and "required all vessels of less than 100 tons entering the Bahamas from Haiti to clear customs and immigration at Matthew Town, Inagua" (106). These new regulations were created to discourage continued Haitian migration to the Bahamas, but Haitians found ways to circumvent the new legislation and their numbers increased. Subsequently, the Bahamian government mounted additional repatriation campaigns in 1980–1981, 1985–1987, and 1992–1994.[8] These campaigns and legal safeguards have also alienated potential future Bahamian citizens: Bahamians of Haitian descent.

Article 6 of the Bahamian Constitution notes that every person born in the Bahamas after July 9, 1973, shall become a national citizen of the Bahamas at the date of his or her birth if at that date either of his or her parents is a citizen of the Bahamas (Treco 2002). Based on this article and subsequent acts, Haitians, or any other foreigners migrating to the Bahamas, cannot become citizens. They can become either a permanent resident with limited rights or legalized through work permits that are renewed through a Bahamian who might sponsor them.

Children born to non-Bahamian parents are not citizens of the Bahamas, which means that they do not have the same rights that accompany the privilege of being a citizen. The children of permanent residents, and documented and undocumented workers are ascribed the nationality of their parents at birth by the Bahamian state. With regard to the child of a Haitian union, the Haitian Constitution does not recognize them as Haitian citizens either because a person must be born on Haitian soil to obtain Haitian citizenship. Therefore, with the Bahamas following the *jus sanguinis* (citizenship determined by one or both parents being citizens of a country) principle of nationality law, and Haiti following the *jus soli* (right of a person born in a territory of a country to nationality or citizenship) principle, children born of non-Bahamian citizens in the Bahamas who fall under these categories are legally neither Bahamian nor Haitian; they are stateless. In Bahamian society, they are ascribed Haitian nationality through a Bahamian certificate of identity. Although recognized socially as Haitian, they are not legally Haitian because they do not have Haitian birth certificates or passports. Therefore, the Bahamian state creates new Haitians through Bahamian constitutional law and its enforcement within Bahamian society.

Bahamian Identity and the Haitian Other

As the result of immigration acts, Bahamian constitutional law, the specter of raids, detention and deportation, and anti-Haitian prejudice that waxes and wanes in moments of economic uncertainty, many Haitians in the Bahamas live in relative social isolation. By withdrawing into Haitian communities and settlements and minimizing contact with Bahamians after work hours, undocumented Haitians increase their chances of working and living in the Bahamas longer without being arrested. The fact that many Haitians who have lived in the Bahamas for years speak little to no English reflects the degree of their social isolation. The unwillingness of the Bahamian government to assist in their integration, and a failure among Bahamian and Haitian voluntary associations and institutions to address language deficiencies among Haitians, exacerbates this isolation.

Haitians seemingly accept their mistreatment and economic exploitation. Haitian construction workers do not protest, for example, when they do a week's worth of work and go unpaid because their employers threaten them with deportation. Haitians are arrested and detained in Bahamian prisons for being undocumented and many fall victim to extortion by Bahamian authorities and sometimes pay between five hundred to two thousand dollars to be released. Haitians also remain segregated from Bahamians due to anti-Haitian sentiment that pervades all ages, classes, and sectors of Bahamian society. This anti-Haitian sentiment is more than everyday prejudice. Bahamian fears about the Haitian "other" constitute an integral ingredient in contemporary constructions of Bahamian identity.

Bahamian identity has a diverse base that contains African, American, British, Gullah, and Haitian elements and stems from a history of slavery, migration throughout the Caribbean, and in-migration from other areas of the Caribbean. Bahamian culture also shares factors with other cultures within the region that situate it in a larger African diaspora. An event called the Junkanoo festival, Bahamian Creole, and Bahamian storytelling (which reflects the legacy of oral history and literature from West and Central Africa) are examples of a culture that has African origins (Johnson 2000, 17).

An important element that undergirds Bahamian fears of Haitians, and constitutes a part of contemporary Bahamian identity, is a long-standing resentment of outsiders and foreigners in the Bahamas. As historian Howard Johnson (2000, 17) observes, resentment of the outsider is a long-standing tradition within Bahamian culture and provides an element of cohesion within a society that has long been separated according to class, color, and race.[9] This distrust of foreigners can be traced to the 1920s, when skilled West Indian laborers arrived to work in the growing tourist industry. Bahamian xenophobia during that period culminated in 1926, when the flow of West Indian laborers was curtailed due to a decrease in opportunities. This type of resentment has carried over to the contemporary period and is reflected in the tensions between Bahamians and Haitians, the largest immigrant group in the nation. As the Haitian population grows, its perceived size feeds into xenophobic fears shared by many Bahamians.

In a joint College of the Bahamas and International Organization for Migration study on Haitian migration to the Bahamas, a review of Bahamian print media from 2003 to 2005 demonstrated how the media contribute to the creation of an atmosphere hostile to Haitians and affirm the hegemonic belief that Haitians are a dangerous internal enemy. According to the review, over half the media reports reviewed concerned the capture, arrest, detention, or return of Haitian nationals. Newspaper articles addressed issues about housing and living conditions, health, environment, migrant smuggling, and the question of citizenship for Bahamian-born children of Haitian nationals. Moreover, there were few feature articles about the resident Haitian community or articles that could promote positive Haitian-Bahamian relations. Overall, the review concluded that the Bahamian media portrays the Haitian migrant population in a way that heightens its perceived threat by the migrants, and the public's perception of the size of the population as very large—anywhere from twenty-five thousand to ninety-five thousand or more Haitians in a country of only some three hundred thousand (College of the Bahamas 2005, 5). The Haitian population actually ranges from thirty thousand to sixty thousand people.

Bahamian anxiety about Haitians in their country also stems from Bahamian views of Haitians as having a different history and language. Ultimately, these perceived cultural differences provide an example and reminder of what Bahamians are not. As historian Michael Craton argues (1995, 284):

> The Bahamian ideal of civilization is based upon economic well-being and progress, and depends on social accommodation not conflict. Alternating economic fortunes had given them an ingenious adaptability, and shared circumstances a unique combination of independence, interdependence and outright dependency, that (to their own mind at least) compromises neither pride nor an innate pacifism. Even the achievement of majority rule and political independence were achieved through "quiet revolutions."
>
> Haitians, on the other hand, are francophone large islanders, familiar with mountains and rivers, essentially peasants, with a long and proud history of independence born in revolution and sustained through struggle. They are perceived by Bahamians as less creolized than themselves, more African, unmodernized, superstitious, fatalistic, emotional and at least potentially violent.

In his work on ethnic groups and boundaries, anthropologist Frederick Barth emphasizes a view of ethnicity that deemphasizes the shared culture of a people as an important way of understanding ethnicity. Barth (1969) stresses that sentiments of communality are defined in opposition to the perceived identity of other racial and ethnic groups. Barth's definition comes to life in the Bahamian context. That is, Bahamians gain a stronger sense of their own ethnicity through their opposition to Haitians. In consideration of Craton's comparison between Bahamians and Haitians, it is clear that Bahamians stereotype Haitians as violent migrants from a country that seemingly cannot rule itself and, most importantly, think that Haitians bring chaos and disorganization with them to the Bahamas. By extension, Haitians supposedly contain the potential to destroy Bahamian societal stability and economic prosperity. Bahamians, on the other hand, are civilized by nature, because they have achieved independence in a "quiet revolution," unlike Haitians, who used guerilla warfare, guns, machetes, and Vodou to gain their independence.

A Bahamian woman named Eloise articulated this view of Haitians. Trained in business in the United States, Eloise got her first taste of American racism while attending undergraduate school in Minnesota. When the patriarch of her family passed away, she put her dreams of being an artist and owning her own farm on hold to assist in her family's business. Eloise held strong views about Haitians and other immigrants in the Bahamas that resonate with the Bahamian view of Haitians that historian Michael Craton articulates. Even though she knew that I was of Haitian descent, Eloise did not hold back her critique:

[Haitians are] thin-skinned, aggressive. . . .

When they see something they want, they go for it. Bahamians are more passive, more laid back. The thing I gotta say about every other country that comes to the Bahamas, they do have this aggressive drive. When they want something, they go for it. They don't stop until they get it. You can have, say a Haitian that came here (to Nassau) maybe six years ago with nothing except the clothes on their back. Now they're driving a Mercedes-Benz. That's happened before. That's happened in lots of cases. Now what they chose to do in that meantime to get that Mercedes-Benz, well I can't speculate. But when they have something in their mind that they want something, they get it.

. . . [There's] also a streak of violence in them. . . . For instance, squatting on property, okay? Once you produce your paper saying that this is my property, a lot [of] times you have problems getting Haitians off your land. We had some construction workers stationed here at one point and they were hired to clear off a certain portion of land that was inhabited by illegal Haitians, alright? And they went to their job and they were surrounded with a lot of men with cutlasses [machetes] telling them that's now their property and they're not gonna do anything on that property. It's clearly not their property. They're there illegally. These guys are just there to do a job. It's that sort of way. Whenever they want it, whether it's by passive or violent means, it will be gotten one way or the other for the most part.[10]

Eloise, a Bahamian, constructs herself as the antithesis of the Haitian: docile and polite. On the other hand, she views Haitians as aggressive intruders who also have a "streak of violence in them." What I found fascinating about her description of Bahamians was her use of the adjectives *passive* and *laid back*. Bahamians can certainly be described as laid back and passive but this is a component of a situational identity employed by Bahamians at their jobs at casinos, resorts, hotels, and restaurants. This situational identity is used in the context of serving primarily white tourists who spend their foreign dollars to be served by docile, grinning black people with tropical drinks (Strachan 2002). Outside of tourist spaces, though—for example, on buses, in clubs, and in the kitchens of restaurants that cater to tourists from North America—Bahamian behavior can be described in similar terms that Eloise uses to describe Haitians. Her comments also suggest that Haitians are violent by nature.

Bahamians of Haitian Descent

Although the progeny of Haitians in the Bahamas are neither legal Haitian nor Bahamian citizens, culturally, they are both Bahamian and Haitian and are referred to at times as "Haitian-Bahamian" in the media and in Bahamian society.[11] The hyphenation of their ethnic identities represents an indignity to many of the Haitian children born in the Bahamas because there is only one preferred nationality, Bahamian, and this is closed to them. Any other identity means being less than a full citizen of the Bahamas, and Haitian nationality almost guarantees downward mobility in Bahamian society.[12] Subsequently, Bahamians of Haitian descent are viewed—and generally referred to—as Haitian in Bahamian society, and they are marginalized in similar yet differing ways from their parents and relatives, who are from Haiti. But some actually succeed in becoming Bahamian citizens.

There is a loophole in Article 7 (1) of the Bahamian constitution that allows some Bahamians of Haitian descent to become Bahamian citizens:

> A person born in the Bahamas after 9th July 1973 neither of whose parents is a citizen of the Bahamas shall be entitled, upon making application on his attaining the age of eighteen years or within twelve months thereafter in such manner as may be prescribed, to be registered as a citizen of The Bahamas:
>
> Provided that if he is a citizen of some country other than the Bahamas he shall not be entitled to be registered as a citizen of the Bahamas under this Article unless he renounces his citizenship of that other country, takes the oath of allegiance and makes and registers such declaration of his intentions concerning residence as may be prescribed. (Bahamas Constitution 1973, 10)

Many Bahamians of Haitian descent spend a lifetime as aliens in the country of their birth. Consequently, it is understandable that the children of Haitians who become Bahamian citizens are sometimes unpatriotic and do not respect the nation of their birth. A young Bahamian woman of Haitian descent I interviewed described the moment when she finally received her Bahamian passport, a material symbol of an elusive nationality and full citizenship in the Bahamas. She indicated that she had no respect for it. In fact, she admitted that she threw her passport around her bedroom regularly and sat on it repeatedly. The laws intended to keep the Bahamas for Bahamians thus result in the Bahamian state producing subjects who are unpatriotic and potentially disloyal.

As a result of laws that marginalize them, Haitian migrants and their progeny use various strategies to survive the hostile social climate of the Bahamas. Like their Haitian counterparts in the Dominican Republic, Guadeloupe, and the United States, Haitians in the Bahamas identify with Haiti to cope with discrimination and exploitation as well as to critique Bahamian culture and society (Brodwin 2003a). Religion, with the church serving as the preeminent institution that addresses Haitian concerns, also plays an important role for Haitians in the Bahamas. The practices of Catholicism, Protestantism, and Vodou provide Haitians with a *bourad* (boost) in their daily lives in a foreign country (Rey and Stepick 2010). Prayer provides hope that undocumented Haitians will continue to go undetected in the Bahamas, and that *Bondyè* (God) will find them a job, protect their clandestine travel to the United States, or ameliorate life in Haiti so that they can return. In the Bahamas, Haitian church participation is a collective mechanism; it allows Bahamians of Haitian descent who shun Haitian culture because of its negative perception in Bahamian society to learn Haitian Creole and Haitian customs, and to acquire a distinctly Haitian Catholic or Protestant religious habitus. Participation in Haitian Protestant denominations also allows Haitians and their progeny in the Bahamas to affirm a Haitian identity free of societal stereotypes within the context of a Christian Bahamas.

Although they reluctantly identify as Haitian, the social identities of Bahamians of Haitian descent are tenuous at best. Dr. Antoine Saint Louis, head pastor of Victory Chapel Church of the Nazarene, attested in an interview that the Haitian children of the Bahamas "hate the nationality of their parents" because of how Haitian nationality relegates them to the bottom of Bahamian society. Members of this group, who have lived most if not all of their lives in the Bahamas, remarked that school, the leading site of their interaction and socialization as Bahamians, is the main site where their marginalization is felt. In fact, their experiences at school have prevented many from publicly identifying as Haitian. For some children, being teased about their Haitian identity is so hard at times that they get into physical altercations with bullies. One young woman I interviewed noted that she stayed away from school for most of an entire year because of the incessant teasing from her Bahamian classmates.[13]

Since "Haitian-Bahamians" are culturally Bahamian, the only factor that reveals the nationality ascribed to them by the Bahamian state is their surnames (such as Louis, Santilien, or Saint-Juste). But even their names can be altered to reflect their Bahamianness. Bahamians of Haitian descent change their names, sometimes even legally, to escape the marginalization that accompanies the discovery of their nationality. For example, a Haitian male whose name is Antoine becomes Anton. Haitian women's names like Antonine and Nadege become Antonette and Nadia in Bahamian society. This quest for successful adaptation sometimes results in ethnic suicide, where Bahamians of Haitian descent cover up the Haitian part of their ethnic origin and present themselves to the world solely as Bahamian (Stepick 1998, 64).

Reginald, a Bahamian of Haitian descent who attended Victory Chapel Church of the Nazarene at the time of our interview, received his Bahamian passport at the age of twenty-eight; ten years after he had applied for it. He recounted the humiliation he felt in high school when a Haitian classmate revealed that he was Haitian in class one day:

Brother . . . the hiding of the identity is because I wanted to get along with the other students, you know? I had a reputation in high school and I thought that the reputation that I had . . . if I let these people know that I am of Haitian descent, if I let them know I was Haitian, if they ever see me talking Creole anywhere it made me feel that they wouldn't be friends with me anymore, you know. But when I get in eleventh grade, and [met] this girl named Sophia, she probably came from another school, she wasn't in our set.[14] . . . Her and this other girl, used to tease me each and every day. [This other girl] used to have it like this [then he pronounces his full name in Haitian Creole as she did]: *"Rejinal! Rejinal!"* I used to say, "Don't call me that! My name Reginald! Don't call me that!" She would say, "Oh, you afraid? You don't want nobody to know your parents Haitian, eh? You don't talk Creole?" I say, "I don't talk Creole! I talk English!" She said, "What you hidin'?" And she just yell it out, "Everybody, Reginald is Haitian!" And everybody had turned around. "You lie! You lie! You lie!" I had my head down for that whole day. I got mad at that girl. After school I cuss her out. I told her everything that I possibly could think of.[15]

Although some Bahamians of Haitian descent have chosen to cloak their Haitian identity as a way to avoid psychological and physical violence and as an adaptive strategy in Bahamian society, some have fought back against their detractors and have become more vocal as an oppressed group while publicly identifying as Haitian (St. Jacques 2001). Many turn to their church, as an outlet for their troubled existence; church participation and conversion thus becomes a way Bahamians of Haitian descent can reconcile their second-class citizenship and secure a form of Haitian identity free of Bahamian social stigma.

Haitians and Bahamians of Haitian descent are subject to laws and a social system in a nation that segregates them and relegates them to an underclass that grows due to continued Haitian migration to the Bahamas and virtually no progress in their incorporation into Bahamian society. Some Haitians are largely complicit in their exploitation and oppression, neither resisting nor challenging their treatment in Bahamian society. Bahamians of Haitian descent use a variety of techniques to resist downward mobility. Some Bahamians of Haitian descent adapt to the hostile social climate and denounce laws that render them stateless in the Bahamas. Others alter their names so that they sound less Haitian as a way of concealing their Haitian heritage. Others openly speak Haitian Creole in public and emphasize their Haitian roots while embracing their Bahamian roots. Overall, Bahamians of Haitian descent underline that the Bahamas is the country of their birth and some continue to press for full inclusion in Bahamian society.

Protestant churches have become the leading institution that addresses the needs of Haitian migrants. Chapter 3 discusses the role of Protestant churches in the lives of Haitian migrants and the Haitian Protestant transnational elements at play in this diasporic religious community.

3

Pastors, Churches, and Haitian
Protestant Transnational Ties

While living in New Providence, I used jitneys to get to church services, interviews with informants, and interdenominational religious gatherings where evangelical churches throughout the Haitian community met to worship at various times of the year. If I wanted to get to Victory Chapel Church of the Nazarene and New Haitian Mission Baptist Church, I would take the 7a bus route. At the beginning of my study of Haitian Protestantism in the Bahamas, I thought those churches were probably two of a handful of Haitian Protestant churches on the island. To my surprise, I would later find out that there were numerous Haitian Protestant churches just along the 7a bus route.

With the help of Brother Frantz, a Bahamian of Haitian descent who attended Victory Chapel Church of the Nazarene, I counted eight Haitian Protestant churches along the 7a bus route: As the bus turns off of Bay Street onto Kemp Road you will see Kemp Road Alliance Church and Prayer and Faith Ministries. The bus then turns onto Wulff Road, where Jerusalem Baptist Church is located, and then left onto Minnie Street, where you will find Victory Chapel Church of the Nazarene.[1] As the bus continues along Minnie Street, you can exit and visit Last Days Gospel Center. Then the bus turns right onto Balfour and you can get off before it passes Palm Beach Street where New Haitian Mission Baptist Church is located. When the 7a reaches East Street you will find Metropolitan Church of the Nazarene and a French Seventh-Day Adventist Church, as well as other Haitian Protestant churches in the nearby Grove area. Other churches that are not along this particular bus route include

International Tabernacle of Praise Ministries, the third church featured in this ethnography, as well as Calvary Baptist Church, Carmichael Evangelical Church, and Emmäus Baptist Church. In 2005, when I began my fieldwork, Haitian pastors estimated the number of Haitian Protestant churches to be twenty or more. As of 2012 the number had increased to at least forty-two.[2]

Historically, Haitians in the Bahamas tended to identify religiously as Catholics. Many Haitians migrate from Haiti as Catholics and practice Catholicism in the different countries in the Haitian diaspora, such as Canada and the United States. Geographer Dawn Marshall (1979, xiii) remarked over three decades ago that the typical Haitian migrant in the Bahamas was "almost certainly a Roman Catholic," but in a 2005 International Organization of Migration report, the majority of Haitians in the Bahamas identified as Protestant. This fact suggests that there is a new religious majority among Haitians in the Bahamas who practice Protestant forms of Christianity.

In an interview with Eliezer Regnier, a Bahamian attorney of Haitian descent, historian Michael Craton (1995, 275) discussed four factors as to why Haitians are converting to Protestant forms of Christianity like Baptist, Nazarene, and Pentecostal faiths in the Bahamas: "The factors that influence Haitian religious conversion to Protestantism forms are targeting from well-funded evangelists, opportunities for participation and leadership, greater encouragement of spiritualist worship than found in the Bahamian Catholic Church, and conversion as an integration strategy into the Christian Bahamas." While these factors may influence Haitian religious conversion to different forms of Protestantism, an underlying assumption in Regnier's statement is that Haitians who migrate to the Bahamas are not Protestant Christians. This may have been true in 1995, when Craton published his article (then one of the few scholarly resources on Haitians in the Bahamas); in my research in three Haitian Protestant churches in New Providence and in numerous interviews in the larger Haitian Protestant community, however, I found that the overwhelming majority of Haitians in my sample had been baptized before they touched Bahamian soil.[3] In fact, only three of the twenty-five Protestants from Haiti whom I interviewed (12 percent) had converted in New Providence. The remaining 88 percent had converted and been baptized in Haiti. In addition to the Haitian practice of Protestant Christianity before migration to the Bahamas, other causes have to be considered for a complete understanding of the practice of Haitian Protestantism in the Bahamas.

Why Haitians Go to Protestant Churches in the Bahamas

Aside from the factors enumerated by Craton (1995), migrant participation at Haitian Protestant churches in the Bahamas is influenced by two key factors. The first is the migrants' desire to maintain their religious practices before immigrating to the Bahamas. This desire is reflected in a Haitian Creole phrase used by many of my research consultants to describe what they sought from Haitian Protestant churches in New Providence. They wanted to go to a church where they would *santi prezans Bondyè* (feel the presence of God). Others used phrases such as *levanjil* (the Gospel) and *lapawòl Bondyè* (the word of God) to describe the type of church at which they preferred to worship. The other influencing factor is directly related to the Bahamian hierarchical social structure and how it shapes the context within which Haitian migrants operate.

As noted earlier, the church is arguably more important to the Bahamian social fabric than school, government, or often even the family. As Dr. Antoine Saint Louis, head pastor of Victory Chapel Church of the Nazarene, remarked:

> The churches play an important role in the lives of Haitians here and those born of Haitian parentage because the church is the only thing about 90 percent of Haitians see as hope. Hope for everything because they feel that

they can depend on [the] church. So the church plays an important role. The church is not only a spiritual entity. The church becomes the father, mother, spiritual, social, financial . . . the church meets all of their needs. They depend on the church to meet their needs.[4]

Glimpses of the structure of Bahamian society illuminate, in part, why the church plays a vital role in the lives of Haitians.

As previously discussed, Bahamian society is structured in a manner that benefits Bahamians, often at the expense or through the exclusion of non-Bahamians. This forces Haitians in the Bahamas, many of whom are undocumented migrants, to withdraw into their own communities. While many Haitians migrate to the Bahamas with the intent of continuing the religious practices that they started in Haiti, the strong Christian religious culture of the Bahamas affects the country's social and power structure. As a result, Haitian Catholic and Protestant churches become the chief institutions that serve the various needs of Haitians in the Bahamas. This, in turn, is an incentive for Haitian migrants in the Bahamas who did not practice Protestantism in their premigratory lives to attend church. As Pastor Saint Louis noted:

Like you said, most of those people that come from Haiti were already Protestant, they were already Christian. And those who are here, they're here in the church every day. This country is a religious country so they accept Jesus as their personal savior. To them that is the number one key. They are genuine and have changed their lives.

And some of them come to church because of the culture [in the Bahamas]. You go to the hospital they will ask you, "What church do you go to?" Wherever you go they will ask you what church. So some of us [Haitians] go to church because of that also.

They don't go to church because they're imitating other people but because of circumstances, they are in church. For example, like I was saying you go somewhere [in the Bahamas] and they ask you, "What church you go to?" You can't say, "I don't go to church." You know, you go apply for something and you can't say, "I don't go to church." Everybody wants to find someplace. So they will say they go to church.[5]

The Three Pastors and Their Churches

I decided to study Haitian Protestantism at New Haitian Mission Baptist Church, Victory Chapel Church of the Nazarene, and International Tabernacle of Praise Ministries Inc. due to the connections that made my research possible. The main person who facilitated my entry into New Providence's Haitian Protestant community was my uncle, Dr. Soliny Védrine, head pastor of Boston Missionary Baptist Church. He is a central figure in the growth of Haitian churches in Boston. He evangelizes among Haitians in Boston and performs mission work in the Bahamas, the Dominican Republic, Haiti, St. Martin, and elsewhere. He is also a pivotal figure in Haïti Vision Du Troisième Centenaire (HAVIDEC), a cooperative movement among Haitian Protestant churches, denominations, and organizations in Haiti and its diaspora that seeks to bring about a spiritual deliverance of Haiti in its third century of existence. And he was part of a missionary group that went to the village of Ti Rivye de Jakmel (Little River, Jacmel) in Haiti in 2002, the same group I joined when I conducted my exploratory research about Protestantism in Haiti.[6]

In 2004, I sent out a survey to Haitian Baptist churches throughout the United States. Among those who responded were three pastors who wrote that they performed mission work in the Bahamas. Additionally, my uncle informed me that he helped to organize an annual international crusade of Haitian Protestants in the Bahamas and that there was a sizeable Haitian Protestant population there. Based on this information, I chose the Bahamas as the country where I would conduct the research for this study.[7] Upon my arrival in New Providence and using my uncle's numerous contacts, I approached Dr. Chérélus Exanté, head pastor of New Haitian Mission Baptist Church of New Providence. My uncle and Dr. Exanté started the tradition of Haitian Protestant international crusades in the Bahamas.

Dr. Soliny Védrine pictured with his wife, Mrs. Emmeline Védrine, at Boston Missionary
Baptist Church, Boston, Massachusetts, September 2009.

Dr. Exanté and New Haitian Mission Baptist Church

Born in Bassin Bleu, outside of Port-de-Paix in Northern Haiti, Dr.
Exanté was raised in a Protestant Christian family and moved to Port-
au-Prince at the age of nine for further schooling. Living in the Delmas
neighborhood in the home of a cousin, he went to a close-by Baptist
church. According to Pastor Exanté, his family in Port-au-Prince was
not Protestant but they did not sway him from his faith and he attended
church with some neighbors. Although he went to Baptist churches and
schools, Dr. Exanté dreamed of becoming a Catholic priest when he was
younger and played games where he would serve as the priest. Once he
began to understand the word of God through a Baptist interpretation
of the Holy Bible, his aspirations and goals changed.

Although he was raised in a Protestant Christian family, Dr. Exanté
did not make the decision to accept Jesus Christ as his personal savior

until he was ten years old. His conversion occurred at a Protestant school when a pastor came to his room, preached, and then asked the children if anyone wanted to give their heart to Jesus. He would stay at his Baptist church in Port-au-Prince for another fifteen years until he attended Pentecostal Unis, which had a prestigious seminary. He eventually enrolled in it to become a pastor.

Dr. Exanté was baptized at his Baptist church in Port-au-Prince in 1963. He had two dreams in his youth that he believes led him to become a pastor. Dreams are a medium that many Haitian Protestants believe *Bondyè* uses to transmit messages and instructions to them. In these dreams, Exanté believed that God was conveying a message to him about his future, that he would one day lead people:

That's a long story. For example, I loved God and I loved church. And finally, one day I was sleeping and I saw myself with my father. We were on a road. And a big truck was coming toward us and the truck had a man inside it who was as big as a church; bigger than a church. My father ran away. . . . He left me in the road by myself. When I looked [down] I had a machete in my hand. I went and cut off the head of the man and then I took gasoline . . . from the truck and poured it all over the man and then I struck a match, [lit him on fire,] and then he died. And then all the people who were running away [from the giant man] came to see what [had] happened, and they took me—this was when I was eleven years old—and everyone lifted me in the air, the same way in the story of Goliath versus David, and then [the dream ended]. I didn't think about it anymore because I didn't understand [the dream].

Then another time when I went to sleep in the same place, I saw a bunch of soldiers with me on a large mountain. We went up, up [the mountain] and we got near the top. The route we were following was very narrow and it was only me and the soldiers who could climb. And when we arrived, I saw the soldiers started to fall back. But I made it to the top of the mountain, and then there was a person who put me there. The person said, "Look to your right. Look to your left. Look in front of you.

Look behind you. You are supposed to lead all of the directions you are looking in. You are a leader."[8]

Later in his life Dr. Exanté realized that it was God who spoke to him through these dreams, conveying that the young man would become a pastor. While in his teens he taught Sunday school. At the age of twenty he went to a seminary and truly believed that he did not choose his current path but that God chose it for him.

Dr. Exanté migrated to the Bahamas in 1982 to be a pastor at Emmäus Baptist Church. According to him, he remained at Emmäus until a disagreement within the church forced him to leave Emmäus and start a new church called New Haitian Mission Baptist Church (New Mission). There were only a few churches in the community at that time (seven or eight by his estimate), and Dr. Exanté started his fledgling institution in a small, pink house next to the site where New Mission stands today. In 2005 New Haitian Mission Baptist Church celebrated its eighteenth anniversary and was the first church where I participated in services, *lajènes* meetings, and special church events. The church averaged about two hundred to two hundred and fifty congregants at Sunday morning services. The majority of the congregants were adults from Haiti who conducted their worship services on the second floor of the church. The first floor of the church held the Sunday school and a youth church service for children of elementary school age. The first floor also contained the head pastor's office, a kitchen, and other rooms. Church members could be a part of the choir and younger church members could participate in *lajènes*.

At the time of my fieldwork, New Haitian Mission Baptist Church had no official doctrine but combined different elements of Haitian Protestantism that I recognized from elsewhere in my transnational study of the religion, which included data and observations in Haiti, the Bahamas, and the United States (including Boston, St. Louis, and Kansas City). New Mission's Sunday school teachers used a text created by UEBH that contains lessons that cover important issues to the Baptist faith such as

New Haitian Mission Baptist Church, June 2012.

conversion, baptism by full immersion in water, and communion. All lessons are supported with references to the Holy Bible.

But unlike other UEBH churches in Haiti, New Mission also had an energetic worship and praise portion of their services. This is because many congregants want to participate in a livelier church service (*tet mare*, Pentecostal-style service), not a church service that lacks emotion (*touloutoutou*, puritanical Protestant-style service). Dr. Exanté explained this distinction when I asked him to describe the differences between the Baptist church he attended in his youth and the Pentecostal church he began to attend when he was living in Haiti:

> The difference is that [the denominations] work together. Baptists work with the Church of God [Pentecostals]. . . . Baptists focus on teaching and the Church of God focuses on teaching and prayer and they have a more exciting worship and praise portion of their services. That means that now the Baptist church has realized that it is *an reta* [late; behind the times]. So,

that means the Baptist church is very cold [*fret*] when it comes to worship and praise now.[9]

Many of the features found at New Mission were also found at Victory Chapel Church of the Nazarene, headed by Dr. Antoine Saint Louis.

Dr. Antoine Saint Louis and Victory Chapel Church of the Nazarene

Dr. Antoine Saint Louis was born of Haitian parents in the Bahamas before Bahamian independence, which means he has always been a citizen of the Bahamas. He was sent back to Haiti with his mother and brother, and lived in Saint Louis du Nord from the age of three, returning to New Providence, Bahamas, at the age of twelve. While living in Saint Louis du Nord, he attended a school affiliated with a Baptist church but had not converted. Upon his return to New Providence at the age of twelve, he remarked:

> I came back [to New Providence] on a Friday and I went to school on Monday. I didn't know a word of English. But at that time there was a good relationship between the kids [of Bahamian and Haitian parentage] so I had a good relationship with the kids at school even though I didn't speak English. Where I lived, the children, after school, would teach me how to speak English. That helped me learn English quicker.[10]

Dr. Saint Louis attended Metropolitan Church of the Nazarene, the first Nazarene church established in New Providence, Bahamas, where he converted by accepting Christ as his personal savior at the age of twelve. He recalled that he was serious about his conversion. Because of his Christian principles he would neither smoke cigarettes nor use profanity unlike his peers. He was baptized as a member of the church two years later. Growing up in the church he partook in most church activities, especially those related to Haitian youth such as the church's youth choir and *lajènes*. Metropolitan Church of the Nazarene would remain his home church until the inception of Victory Chapel.

After Dr. Saint Louis graduated from high school, he worked as a carpenter and a water vendor for three years to save money for college. He was accepted to Nazarene Theological College in Trinidad. After he received his degree, he returned to New Providence, broke and without a job. Because of his leadership skills and educational achievements, Dr. Saint Louis was well prepared to lead a church of his own. The following month, he received a call from the the Church of the Nazarene district superintendent requesting that he lead a church where he would preach primarily in English. He prayed about the request and then told the superintendent that there had to be a multicultural church that would meet the needs of the children of Haitians born in New Providence. The superintendent agreed and Victory Chapel Church of the Nazarene was created. Before the church emerged, children of Haitian parentage would go to either an English-speaking church (Bahamian) or a Haitian church where only Haitian Creole and French were spoken. As Saint Louis observed, the Haitian children born in the Bahamas were unable to appreciate their two cultures (Haitian and Bahamian) until a church was created where young people could come and be proud of their parents and their place of birth.[11] Victory Chapel moved to its Minnie Street location in 1995.[12]

Victory Chapel is a one-level church with a sanctuary that can accommodate at least two hundred and fifty people. In addition to its sanctuary, it has other rooms where young Bahamians of Haitian descent attend Sunday school and participate in their own services while an adult service takes place. Unlike New Haitian Mission Baptist Church and International Tabernacle of Praise Ministries, Victory Chapel's congregation at the time of this study was 50 percent Haitian and 50 percent Bahamian of Haitian descent. The congregations at the other churches were overwhelmingly Haitian rather than overwhelmingly Bahamian of Haitian descent. This demographic was reflected in how the services at Victory Chapel were conducted. Sunday morning services were usually bilingual services conducted in Haitian Creole and English.

Additionally, Victory Chapel was the only church in the study that had a band. Live music made a big difference in the worship and praise

Victory Chapel Church of the Nazarene, June 2012.

portion of services by creating an atmosphere where congregants, who danced and sang, were guided by *lasentespri* (the Holy Spirit). Victory Chapel also has many activities and groups for its members. Adult male members of the church can join *gwoup dom* or become a deacon, pastor, or usher. Adult female members can join *gwoup dam* or the women's choir, or lead Sunday school. Those ranging in age from roughly the early teens to the thirties, can join *lajènes*, the church youth group.[13] In addition, there were morning and evening Sunday services, *jènn*, and *etid biblik* (Bible study), which are open to church members of all ages.

Victory Chapel Church of the Nazarene follows the doctrine of the global Nazarene church. Founded in 1908 in Pilot Point, Texas, the Church of the Nazarene is a Protestant Christian church in the Wesleyan-Holiness tradition. Doctrinally, Victory Chapel Church of the Nazarene emphasizes the principles of sanctification and holiness, which are not emphasized at New Mission and International Tabernacle of Praise Ministries. The Wesleyan-Holiness tradition holds that it is not enough for a person to be saved or even baptized as a sign of being a true Christian. A person must continually confess his or her sins and is constantly regenerated as a result of leading a sanctified and holy life.

At the time of this study, Victory Chapel celebrated its seventeenth anniversary. The next church in the study, International Tabernacle of Praise, was a new church at the time and celebrated its first year of existence with its pastor, Kevin Pierre.

Pastor Pierre and International Tabernacle of Praise Ministries

Pastor Kevin Pierre was born of Haitian parents in New Providence, Bahamas, before Bahamian independence in July 1973, which made him a Bahamian citizen; he was thirty-eight years old at the time of our interview in 2005. When he was around three or four years old, his mother was deported to Haiti and she took Kevin to live with his grandparents outside of Au Borgne in northern Haiti, in a place called Ti Bouk (little village) Oboi. Then he was sent to Port-au-Prince to live with his maternal aunt until a pastor—who had met Kevin's mother in New Providence, Bahamas, and had told her about an institution in he was involved in—came to take him to an orphanage in La Pointe des Palmistes in the northern region of the country. By that time Kevin was in his preteens.

Pastor Pierre spoke fondly of his time at the orphanage, where he converted to Protestant Christianity through the Baptist faith and dedicated his life to Jesus Christ:

> One of the things that I remember once I became a Christian was the place [where] I became a Christian: at the orphanage. We had service in the morning. I remember that I became a Christian at the age of fourteen or fifteen, in 1979, I believe, at the age of fourteen. God had spoken to my heart; after I heard a message I went to the superintendent. I told him that I want to give my life to the Lord because I heard a message [called] "Where will you spend eternity when you die?" At a very young age, thirteen or fourteen, I gave my life to the Lord. That was a great move I made in my life, . . . and I never regret it.
>
> And I must say that most of the values, most of the belief[s], . . . most of the philosophy that I share today are from that place, from that orphanage. Hard work, a sense for community work, a sense of love for persons, a sense of love for school and education, I learned that from the orphanage.[14]

Pastor Pierre also articulated what was different about his Catholic upbringing that troubled him and how his conversion to Protestant Christianity satisfied him:

> What wasn't satisfying to me [about Catholicism] is that I remember that in the Catholic faith . . . my longing for Christ was not [ful]filled. My longing for Christ was incomplete, . . . [although] you heard much about Christ coming to save you, Christ loves you. [After conversion] I didn't have to pray to St. Mary or confess my sins; and I remember growing up in the environment of Ti Bouk Oboi when I killed rats and a roach, you had to go to the priest and ask him to forgive you. Before you became

komunye [second stage of maturity in the Catholic faith of Haiti] I had to ask a priest to forgive me because I kill a rat, I kill a roach. I remember those things. But now I know when I become a Christian that I have to go directly to Christ, to Jesus Christ to forgive me for my sins. And really since then I have a priest within when I asked the Lord to enter into my life.[15]

His mother removed Kevin from the orphanage; first she moved him back in with his grandparents in Ti Bouk and then to Cap-Haïtien for schooling until 1986—after dictator Jean-Claude Duvalier fled Haiti aboard an American-chartered jet—when she sent for him to return to New Providence, Bahamas. At that time, the future pastor was nineteen years old.

Speaking only a few words of English upon his arrival, Pastor Pierre began a new life in the Bahamas and attended services at Emmäus Baptist Church. He later became a secretary and teacher in Sunday school. His first paying job was washing cars. He wanted to learn English so he listened to the radio, watched television, and read Bahamian newspapers. In his interview, Pastor Pierre remarked that while living in the Bahamas, he saw firsthand that Haitians were living under substandard conditions and that Bahamians spoke negatively about Haitians in the Bahamas. He wanted to make a contribution to improving the lives of Haitians in the Bahamas and spoke out against the deportation of Haitians and Bahamians of Haitian descent and their overall mistreatment in the Bahamas on the radio and television.

Pastor Pierre recounted that he had a great yearning to work for God even at a young age. He remembered that while attending Emmäus Baptist church, the resident pastor left for the United States and a freemason was supposed to be put in his place. Along with other young Haitians in his congregation, Pastor Pierre blocked the appointment of that pastor because some devout Haitian Protestants believe that freemasonry consists of demonic rituals and is antithetical to Haitian Protestant Christianity. Dr. Ruben Cooper Jr., a Bahamian pastor who is the head of

Mission Baptist Church, was also involved in the selection of a new pastor at Emmäus at that time and saw a great desire within young Kevin to serve the Lord and to help the Haitian people in the Bahamas. Dr. Cooper proposed that he further his education and, to that end, had his secretary help with an application to American Baptist College, a Bible college in the United States where Pastor Pierre was later accepted.

Located in Nashville, Tennessee, American Baptist College, a historically black Bible college, prepares its students for careers in Christian service and trains many Bahamian pastors. Pastor Pierre took courses in English, Baptist Covenant, Evangelism, the New Testament, Theology, Philosophy, Psychology, and the Christian Life of Jesus Christ. During summer breaks he would return to New Providence and attend Mission Baptist Church and continue on a path that would eventually lead to forming his own Haitian Protestant church. Pastor Pierre made friends with a few Bahamians at American Baptist College who would take him anywhere he needed to go while in Nashville and bought necessities for him. However, although Pastor Pierre was a Bahamian citizen, other Bahamian students at American Baptist College who went on to pastor churches in the Bahamas perceived Haitians negatively and ostracized him. Conversely, Pastor Pierre felt accepted by his American peers and professors who were predominantly African American.

Pastor Pierre was one of the few Haitians who attended American Baptist College. He wanted to leave a good impression of Haitians for his peers and professors so he worked hard, earned his General Education Development (GED) diploma, and received a bachelor's degree magna cum laude. After graduation, he returned to New Providence and worked full-time in the ministry at Dr. Cooper's church. Before he had left for his schooling in the United States, Pastor Pierre was a deacon at Mission Baptist Church. He returned to the church as a reverend and was addressed as minister by churchgoers at Mission Baptist Church. During this time Pastor Pierre also worked throughout the Haitian Protestant community, preaching sermons and teaching English classes; he even taught theology in the French (Haitian) section at Atlantic Theological Seminary.

Three years before he left Mission Baptist Church for good, Pastor Pierre started a Thursday night *veydenwi* (prayer service) at his mother's house that was conducted in Haitian Creole. In 2004 the people who were participating in *veydenwi* decided that they wanted to start a church with him as pastor and asked him to search for a permanent location for their new place of worship. Formally founded between July and August 2004, International Tabernacle of Praise Ministries Inc. (ITP) became a reality. As Pastor Pierre explained, "we had few persons from the prayer meetings who came together, in my absence, and they met and they said that 'I think we can find a location to worship God.'"

And so the church found a place close to the main campus of the College of the Bahamas. At that time, ITP was working toward a mission statement and a doctrine. It is a small church with about thirty to forty regular attendees and features people with Catholic, Jehovah's Witnesses, Pentecostal, Baptist, Adventist, and Mormon backgrounds. Although Pastor Pierre comes from a Baptist background, he did not want to open up another Baptist church in the Bahamas (at the time of this study, New Providence already had more than ten Haitian Baptist churches). ITP is an interdenominational church and its worship style is charismatic in nature. Pastor Pierre believed that in order to grow his church, he could not have a traditional Haitian Baptist church service, as he put it, "dead" (*touloutoutou*). He has hopes that ITP will be the basis of an apostolic interdenominational movement among Haitians in New Providence:

You have a lot of Haitians who go to Protestant churches who are not liberated in their mind and their spirit, because they have not accepted the fact it is in giving to God that you are blessed. I told my church that I want to use them as the model of how you can be blessed. I'm touched by the Haitian community. I feel for the Haitian community. I cannot perceive one of my church members being in the Bahamas for twenty years, like my mother, [who has] been in the Bahamas for forty years, and she doesn't have anything that she can identify with in the Bahamas, okay? And you have 80 or 90 percent of Haitians in the Bahamas like that, okay?

International Tabernacle of Praise Ministries, July 2012.

I cannot perceive that. I cannot perceive someone being at my church for five years and unable to understand properly the English language and to be a burden to the government.

I asked the Lord the way he has trained me, the way he has given me the experiences, serving with Pastor Cooper for almost fifteen years, training with him and in the United States. I want to make a difference. I want this ministry to make a difference. I'm not just saying saving souls is the priority but to be able to empower people, my worshippers, in mind, body, and spirit; holistically, socially, spiritually, educationally, and morally. Why form a new church? Because I think that there's a need for another [Haitian] church that is not Adventist, that is not Catholic, that is not Baptist, that is not Church of God but is Apostolic, nondenominational.

Apostolic means that I believe in all the works of the Apostles (the twelve apostles of Jesus Christ), I believe in healing, I believe in speaking in tongues. I believe in all that Baptists believe but I believe in some more. I will not tell [a woman] who is wearing earrings [to church] to go outside. And I won't tell [a woman] who is not wearing earrings or jewelry to stop coming to my church.

I don't want to prevent [women] from coming to worship with me because they [only] have pants [to wear]. . . . My church might have a different view. . . . If a woman like that [wears pants] and comes to worship God, she can come. Most of the Haitian churches would have different views . . . I want to be a Haitian ministry that makes a difference, that makes an impact.[16]

Pastor Pierre defines denominationalism by noting the cultural aspects of charismatic denominations like Pentecostalism, where male and female adherents practice self-denial and austerity. Their piety is represented in the way they dress. Pentecostal women in Haiti tend not to wear makeup or pants in or outside of church. If a woman who has not converted wears makeup, earrings, and pants while visiting ITP, congregants might criticize her, but that is not Pastor Pierre's desire. He wants ITP to be an institution that attempts to transcend the symbolic boundaries that devout Haitian Protestants use to critique the behavior and appearance of Haitians in Haiti and the Bahamas. He believes that the private use of the term *Pwotestan* by some congregants, judgmental attitudes, and denominational differences at ITP could cause a great deal of friction between church attendees and also might discourage first-time visitors from coming back. Pastor Pierre genuinely wants Haitians to come to Jesus because of the positive transformational effects that Protestant Christianity guarantees, as he believes his life story reflects.

Transnational Ties

To view New Mission, Victory Chapel, and ITP as solely part of the larger community of Haitian Protestant churches in the Bahamas would ignore the larger transnational Haitian Protestant context in which these churches are embedded. Transnationalism is a term used within academia to describe cultural phenomena related to national border crossing. To bring some clarity to the concept of transnationalism in their study of transnational immigrant religious networks that are connected to Houston, Texas, sociologists Helen Rose Ebaugh and Janet Saltzman Chafetz (2002, 3) refer to Portes et al. (1999) who limit the use of the term to "occupations and activities that require regular and sustained social contacts over time and across national borders for their implementation." For methodological reasons, Portes et al. define the individual and his or her support networks as the proper unit of analysis when considering transnational activities. They then argue that data collected from individuals makes it possible to delineate the networks of their transnational enterprises. In addition, a researcher can identify the transnational entrepreneurs' counterparts in the home country and garner information to establish the aggregate structural effects of transnational activities.

Using Portes et al.'s formulation, we can view religious activities occurring between Haitian Protestants in the United States and Haitian Protestants in New Providence, Bahamas, as transnational activities. During my fieldwork at New Haitian Mission Baptist Church, Haitian Protestant congregations from Brooklyn, New York, and Philadelphia, Pennsylvania, visited the church and conducted evangelization throughout the Haitian community. They also preached consecutive nights at the church, and performed Haitian gospel music. In addition, evangelists from Boston, Massachusetts, and Miami, Florida, preached at Sunday services while I was there. But Portes et al.'s definition of transnationalism comes to life most vividly through the annual International Crusade.

In May 2005 several hundred Haitian Protestant migrants convened for a week of sermons, worship and praise, and spiritual edification at the Church of God Auditorium on Joe Farrington Road. This event is known officially as the United Evangelistic International Crusade and informally as the International Crusade. Every year the crusade takes place Monday through Sunday and the pastors, church elders, and congregations from Haitian Protestant churches in the community convene nightly.[17] Each night had a different theme, for example, "Youth Night" or "Civic Night," and the crusade took the familiar liturgical form associated with Haitian Protestantism: worship and praise, scripture readings, choir selections, a sermon, hymns, testimonies, and a closing benediction. The Church of God auditorium on Joe Farrington Road holds up to six thousand people and on some nights the auditorium was nearly full.

The crusade has its roots in a transnational relationship between Dr. Soliny Védrine, head pastor of Boston Missionary Baptist Church, and Dr. Chérélus Exanté, head pastor of New Haitian Mission Baptist Church. Dr. Védrine and Dr. Exanté's relationship—which is based on religious affiliation, nationality, and friendship—extends across national borders and is situated in a transnational social field: a terrain of personal networks that connect Haitian Protestants in the United States, the Bahamas, Canada, Haiti, and the Dominican Republic (Glick Schiller and Fouron 2001, 57). In an interview Dr. Védrine discussed how he became involved in evangelical work with Haitians in the Bahamas:

Also in 1993 and in 1994 I was invited to Nassau, Bahamas, by [Dr.] Chérélus Exanté to visit his work there and to see the need of Haitians there.

When I got there it was natural for me to do the work that I do in Boston, to gather Haitian pastors, to pray together, to think what they can do together.[18] We decided to have a fellowship of pastors. I'm working with nineteen pastors in Nassau, Bahamas. By 1996 we started what we were doing in Boston in the Bahamas, a big gospel outreach for a whole week where the gospel is preached every night.[19]

According to Pastor Exanté, the seed for the crusade was planted in 1995 when Exanté visited Védrine's church in Boston. Together they came up with an idea to have the crusade—which includes Haitian Evangelical Protestants from Canada, the Dominican Republic, Haiti, and the United States—to incite spiritual, moral, and economic change among Haitians in the Bahamas.

The crusade also has a service and humanitarian component that takes place during the day. These activities attempt to address the physical and mental health of Haitians living in the Bahamas as well as to provide money for Haitian undergraduate theological training and pastoral seminars for the education of Haitian Protestants who preach the word of God:

But because of [Haitian] needs, we brought a new dimension to our outreaches. We brought doctors and nurses to minister people medically for the whole week. The medical work has been coordinated by Dr. Mirtha Jean and is a key feature in our outreach in the Bahamas since 1996. When she comes she brings a staff of doctors and nurses from Boston and New York. In our last mission she served over one thousand people and gave them medicine and medical advice. Hospitals across the U[nited] S[tates] donated over thirty thousand dollars worth of medical supplies for the mission.

I have also brought seminary students, working toward their master's degrees, there to work with the young people because a lot of the young Haitians are *lost* in Bahamian society and not fully integrated and many of them have gone the wrong way. So the seminary students serve as counselors to them to encourage them to look at life more positively. We have helped some students pay for their tuition to go to college and we want to continue that work. In addition, my wife has been working with pastors' wives, having retreats for them and special conferences. We have invited Haitians from other countries as well. For instance, in 2004 the whole week of gospel outreach in the Bahamas had attracted Haitians from the U[nited] S[tates], from Canada, from Haiti, from the Dominican Republic, and from Jamaica.[20]

What Dr. Védrine refers to as the social dimension of the International Crusade also takes place throughout the Haitian Protestant community found in New Providence. A *klinik* (clinic) is set up at New Haitian Mission Baptist Church and throughout the day Haitians trickle in while an international team of Haitian doctors and nurses check blood pressure, provide consults, and prescribe medicine to patients for an assortment of ailments that go untreated many times due to their undocumented status and poverty.[21]

As I have shown, the Bahamas is home to Haitian Protestants whose religious histories and traditions can be traced back to Haiti, in addition to Haitians who decide to convert to Protestant forms of Christianity for practical purposes. They were already Protestant Christians before they arrived in the Bahamas. The Haitian Protestant community of the Bahamas is part of a transnational Haitian Protestant community that is growing in Haiti and in diasporic locales within the region. This community is situated within a larger transnational social field that shares some of the same beliefs and practices (such as the rejection of Vodou) that unify Haitian Protestant identity across national borders.

Chapter 4 describes the Haitian Protestant liturgy, its form and the various ritual activities that are part of church services. This liturgy and worship style, I will argue, creates a religious environment that induces conversion and maintains devout identities among devout Haitian Protestants in the Bahamas.

4

Haitian Protestant Liturgy

Haitian Protestant liturgy—which consists of praise, worship, hymnody, and sermons—is an integral part of the practice of Haitian Protestant Christianity. Liturgy serves to bind individuals into the body of Christ and is structured in a manner that promotes collective worship while reinforcing hierarchy: At the top is the holy trinity (God, Jesus Christ, and the Holy Spirit), followed by the pastors, deacons, and Sunday school monitors, and then come the members and believers who assemble to worship and praise God at Haitian Protestant churches. Pastors and deacons are authorities within the church who preach, organize, teach, admonish, and counsel church members. A closer look at the worship and praise portion of services, Haitian Protestant hymnody, and sermons illuminates the importance of Haitian Protestant liturgy in helping to create, encourage, and maintain devout Christian identities.

Worship and Praise

Regardless of where Haitian Protestant church services are held—Boston Missionary Baptist Church in Massachusetts, the first French-speaking Baptist Church of Saint Louis, Missouri, Victory Chapel Church of the Nazarene in New Providence, Bahamas, or Pentecostal Unis of Port-au-Prince, Haiti—they all share a similar worship format. Most church services begin with a *culte d'adoration et louange* portion in which adherents worship and praise God through hymns and prayers led by members of the church hierarchy. Haitian Protestant hymnody is usually drawn from Chants d'espérance, a Baptist hymnal used by Haitian Protestant churches within a transnational social field. Many in the congregation memorize the melodies and verses of the hymns, which are in French and Haitian Creole, as well as gospel songs that express similar themes of Christian faith and adoration of the Lord and are sung at church services and other Haitian Protestant events. Haitian Protestants believe in a unique God and in the holy trinity of God, the Son (Jesus Christ), and the Holy Spirit; this God is the creator of everything, redeems and consoles his followers, and is omnipotent (Romain 1986, 222).

The *culte d'adoration* part of the service is sometimes mingled with Bible verses that correspond to the theme of the church service. Aspects of Haitian Protestant church culture—such as the swaying of hands in the air and people calling out, "Amen," "*Beniswa Letènel* [Praise the Lord]," "*Glwa a Dyè* [Glory to God]," and "*Mesi Seyè* [Thank you, Lord]"—are on full display. Some people kneel at the altar in fervent, silent prayer while others stand and sing from their Chants d'espérance hymnals. The *culte d'adoration* portion of the service is followed by additional scripture readings, the performance of more hymns, announcements made by the assistant or head pastor, and the presentation and greeting of visitors. After the church visitors stand up and introduce themselves by name and place of origin, the pastor, a church member, or a visitor (who could be a fellow pastor in the community, an evangelist, or a speaker from overseas) delivers the sermon of the day. The sermon is followed by a call for *moun ki poko konvèti* (people who have not converted to Haitian Protestantism yet) and backsliders to dedicate their lives to Jesus and lead a Christian life. The service concludes with a *benediksyon* (benediction), spoken out loud by a pastor, deacon, or member of the church.

Haitian Protestant Hymnody and Brother Volny

Hymnody, an important feature of Haitian Protestant liturgy, aids in the creation of memorable church experiences that reflect Haitian Protestant culture. Hymnody helps adherents to worship and praise the Lord and lift their spirits. It is important to view the songs that they sing as part of a religious identity that they use in an effort to set themselves apart from Haitian and Bahamian secular life. Migrants sing during the worship and praise portion of services, at prayer meetings, at crusades, revivals and in musical competitions between church groups. During services, at special moments, individual church members may perform a Haitian gospel song or a selection from a hymnal as a way of praising and worshipping God. This form of worship occurred at New Mission and Victory Chapel at times when I attended those churches. It also took place at International Tabernacle of Praise one Sunday, when a church member named Brother Volny sang a song to demonstrate his *krent pou Bondyè* (fear of God) and the life he tries to lead as a *Kretyen*.

Brother Volny was born and raised in La Gonave, an island west of Port-au-Prince, the capital of Haiti, in the town of Anse-a-Galets. At the time of our interview, he had lived in the Bahamas for a year and a few months. Brother Volny was in his mid-thirties and had left Haiti because of the lack of employment opportunities made it difficult for both him and his wife to support their family. Brother Volny recalled that there was a strong Protestant presence in Anse-a-Galets while he was growing up, and he attended the church and school of his uncle who was a Wesleyan minister. He accepted Christ sometime between 1988 and 1989 and was baptized approximately a year later in the same church. Soon after his baptism, he attended a Nazarene church for a brief period before he and his wife decided to attend Bethesda, an independent church unaffiliated with any Protestant denomination. Brother Volny noted that the religious style at Bethesda was similar to the manner that adherents at Pentecostal and charismatic churches worship (Robbins 2004).

At a service I attended at International Tabernacle of Praise, Brother Volny reappeared after an absence of a couple of weeks. Before the sermon was delivered that morning, he stood at the front of the church to testify. Testimonials play an integral part in the conversion stories of adherents and are public declarations in which believers of Jesus Christ stand in front of assemblages and share stories of how they converted or provide an example of the role God played at an important moment in their lives. In some testimonials, God aids a role in avoiding death, preventing misfortune, healing a troubled marriage, and healing illnesses. Deliveries of testimonials among adherents were also common at *jènn* and at the weeklong International Crusade for Haitian Protestants that takes place every May. Anthropologist Susan Harding notes that testimonials—like evangelizing, gospel preaching, spreading the Word, and witnessing—are part of conversion rhetoric. This means that testifying can be seen as "an argument about the transformation of self that lost souls must undergo, and a method of bringing about that change in those who listen to it" (Harding 1987, 167).

That morning at International Tabernacle of Praise we all saw the emotion in Brother Volny's eyes as he stood before the congregation and delivered a passionate speech. As he fought back tears and paused when he was overcome with emotion, he told the congregation that he had been imprisoned in the Carmichael Road detention center for two weeks, and that his family members living in New Providence had paid for his release and that he would have to pay them back. During the course of my research, I heard numerous stories about Haitian men who were arrested and later released from prison. Any undocumented people living in the Bahamas who are arrested are supposed to be deported back to their country of origin. In some of these cases the men who were arrested would resurface at their churches, demonstrating yet another way the Bahamian state ruthlessly exploits Haitians by bribing their prisoners only to arrest them again at a later time.

Brother Volny told the congregation that he sang out of a small Haitian Protestant hymnal during his imprisonment. Singing from the book gave him comfort and strength to have faith in his future by trusting God, fearing God, and placing his unsettled future in God's hands. The song he sang that morning is called "*Jeova Chalom* [Jehovah Shalom]." The title of the song refers to a greeting Haitian Protestants use with each other; its meaning is similar to the greeting *la pe Bondyè avèk ou* (may the peace of God be with you). As tears streamed down his face, and as his voice cracked on certain notes and words, Brother Volny sang decrying his faith to those who would listen.

While Brother Volny sang, members of the church shouted "oh yes" in English, a familiar exclamation in Haitian Protestant churches in New Providence when a hymn or part of a sermon resonates with adherents and they feel a push from inside them to exclaim something. Others clapped and shouted "Amen" and "*Alelouya*" along with each verse that Brother Volny sang. As a whole, the song offers a prime example of the ways in which devout Haitian Protestants can worship and praise as individuals. The performance of the song is also a testament to having faith in God no matter how fearful one might be in the face of danger and uncertainty as an undocumented immigrant in the Bahamas.

Bondyè gen pwogram pou tout pitit li	God has a plan for all of his children
Li sekoure yo le yo anba tray	He helps them when they are tested
Li di fe silans, konfye nan mwen	He tells them, "Be quiet and confide in me
Ou pa gen dwa janm pedi batay	You never have any reason to lose in your battle/fight."

Kè:	*Refrain:*
Jeova Chalom, mwen beni non ou!	Jehovah Shalom, I praise your name!
Jeova Chalom, mwen magnifye ou!	Jehovah Shalom, I magnify you!
Ou se ranpa mwen, espwa lavi mwen,	You are my fortress, my life's hope,
Jeova Chalom, mwen beni non ou!	Jehovah Shalom, I praise your name!

Moun ki pou Bondyè	*Those who are for God*
Pa dwe pè anyen	Need not fear anything
Anyen pap rive w san pèmisyon	Nothing will happen to you without His permission
Kite kè ou an pe piga ou twouble	Let your heart be peaceful, beware of trouble
Menm branch chève nan tet ou konte	Every hair on your head is accounted for and taken care of

Although no one converted that morning, Brother Volny's testimony and performance nevertheless served an important purpose for those who attended. First, he sang at church as a way to express his love and faith in God because of how God guided him through a difficult period in his life. This experience strengthened Brother Volny's faith and fortitude. Moreover, his performance also showed those in attendance whose faith in God might be weak, that they too could be arrested at any time and that they needed to have faith. Overall, Brother Volny's faith in God—as was apparent in his performance and comportment—was a testament to and demonstration of his *krent pou Bondyè*.

Victory Chapel, *Lajènes*, and Songs

An intellectualist analysis of the songs sung by members of this diasporic religious community reveals issues of contestation and resistance among Bahamians of Haitian descent, the progeny of Haitians living in the Bahamas. As mentioned earlier, they are stigmatized and discriminated against by Bahamian society, which identifies them as Haitian, and this frequently causes them to hate the identities the Bahamian state assigns them; it also leads them to find other institutions to address their economic, social, and spiritual needs (St. Jacques 2001). Some Bahamians of Haitian descent attend Bahamian churches and emphasize the Bahamian part of their identities. The majority, though, attend the various Catholic and Haitian Protestant churches in New Providence. One of those churches is the Protestant Victory Chapel Church of the Nazarene, which was created, according to its head pastor, Dr. Antoine Saint Louis, explicitly to minister to Bahamians of Haitian descent. In the earlier years of Victory Chapel, Haitian youth born in the Bahamas made up the majority of the churchgoers. As of 2005 the church's demographic composition was evenly split between Haitians who had migrated to the Bahamas from Haiti and Bahamians of Haitian descent.

On October 28, 2005, I attended a *lajènes* meeting with the intent to recruit more people for my research. Some of the young women were rehearsing a dance that they intended to perform during the annual youth conference; the chorus rehearsed the soprano, alto, tenor, and bass parts of two songs. The first song they rehearsed that night was one that visitors from Haiti had taught the *lajènes* group. The Victory Chapel band consisted of a keyboardist, drummer, and bass player, all of whom were male and ranged in age from their late teens to their mid-twenties. The members of the group were self-taught musicians with a talent for moving effortlessly between different musical styles such as *konpa* and African American gospel. For this song the band accompanied the singers with a reggae rhythm while the chorus sang solely in Haitian Creole:

Mete m nan difè, Seyè (Bis/2x)	*Put me in the fire, Lord (repeat two times)*
Wi mwen vle viv lavi m	Yes I want to live my life
Pou m fe w plèzi	To make you happy
Nan tout bagay	In everything (I do)
Mete m nan difè, Seyè (Bis/2x)	*Put me in the fire, Lord (repeat two times)*
Mwen vle lemonn we	I want the world to see
M ap briye pou ou	That I am shining for you.

The lyrics are straightforward: *Mete m nan difè, Seyè* means that as Christians the members of Victory Chapel's *lajènes* will have their faith tested by *dyab* (the Devil) and other evils of the secular world. *Lajènes* members struggle to lead Christian lives to please God in a country that treats them as second-class citizens. The yearning we find among them is complex and contains different meanings: living their lives within their communities through literal translations of Old and New Testament scriptures, concentrating on the teachings of Jesus Christ as a way to perfect oneself, or focusing on the Nazarene emphases on sanctification and holiness. The song also reflects the youth group's symbolic inclusion into the Christian nation of the Bahamas, where their

Haitianness does not exclude them from participation or relegate them to a spiritual underclass because they are all children of God. Unlike the alienation they experience in Bahamian society, Victory Chapel's *lajènes* are accepted and loved by God and will become citizens of God's Kingdom as long as they continue to lead Christian lives. Then Bahamians, who profess to be Christian, should be able to accept the progeny of Haitians in the Bahamas. The song ends with *Mwen vle lemonn we m ap briye pou ou* (I want the world to see that I am shining for you), a brilliant example of God's hope for humans on Earth, set to a reggae rhythm. The song also conveys a message of hope in that being obedient to God and doing God's work on Earth as a shining Christian example will eventually lead to the citizenship of *lajènes* in heaven and full inclusion into Bahamian society.[1]

The Victory Chapel *lajènes* group also incorporates aspects of the secular in their religious performances. Reggae (dancehall reggae) is ubiquitous on the island of New Providence. It can be heard on the buses that are used by the Bahamian working class and Haitian underclass; it emanates from the shops that line the poorer neighborhoods of New Providence and from the bars that the Bahamian working class patronizes; and it fills the clubs that are frequented by tourists and Bahamians. The choice of this song, including its accompanying rhythm and musical style, refers to a key aspect of how Bahamians of Haitian descent, as opposed to devout Haitian Protestant migrants, practice Protestant Christianity: through the appropriation and incorporation of secular and religious cultural forms from the Bahamas, Jamaica, African American religious culture, and Christian global media. This desire to construct a religious self that is calibrated to local social conditions in the Bahamas becomes apparent in the Victory Chapel *lajènes* rehearsal of *Na va triyonfe* ("We Shall Overcome").

After *Mete m nan difè* was rehearsed numerous times, the *lajènes* president wrote the lyrics for "We Shall Overcome" on a blackboard located in the sanctuary—first in English and then in Haitian Creole for the *lajènes* to perform for their youth conference and group competition:

We shall overcome (repeat)
We shall overcome someday
Down in my heart
I do believe
We shall (repeat)
We shall overcome someday

The Victory Chapel band accompanied the chorus in a style inspired by gospel music created by African Americans in the United States. The group of sopranos, altos, and tenors rehearsed the song in English and then sang the Haitian Creole translation:

Na va triyonfe (repeat)
Na va triyonfe yon jou
Andedan kè m
Mwen telman kwe
Na va (repeat)
Na va triyonfe yon jou

When the Victory Chapel *lajènes* sang "We Shall Overcome" in English and Haitian Creole their use of this song, which is arguably the signature song of the African American civil rights movement in the United States, was intentional in that it related directly to their hopes within the context of the Bahamas. As African Americans fought for full inclusion and rights as American citizens in the United States, Bahamians of Haitian descent see a historical counterpart to their daily struggles for integration, self-determination, acceptance, and incorporation as citizens with full rights in Bahamian society. The accompanying music the band played was in an African American gospel style that is part of the Christian religious culture in the Bahamas and draws on African American religious traditions and cultural forms to create a representation of a religious self. The performance of "We Shall Overcome" also reflected the hybridized identities of *lajènes*: they are culturally Bahamian and Haitian, although the Bahamian state at times violently enforces and privileges Bahamian nationality over all others. The rehearsal and performance of "We Shall Overcome" by the Victory Chapel *lajènes* also highlighted the yearning for a movement for equality that starts in their church. Looking back to the achievements of the civil rights movement in the United States, which was headed by African Americans from the Protestant Christian tradition in the American South, Bahamians of Haitian descent hope that the Bahamian state will one day make them citizens without being stigmatized as Haitian and that they will one day avoid the dehumanizing and seemingly paradoxical process of application for citizenship in a country that they were born in.

The appropriation of an African American musical style by the progeny of Haitian migrants to address their treatment, along with other musical styles (such as reggae) and forms of dress within the region (such as hip-hop), also are calibrated to local conditions and are in opposition to the cultural and religious traditions of the generation of their parents. In her study of the efficacy of fundamentalist Baptist rhetoric among the US political action group Moral Majority, anthropologist Susan Harding (1987) acknowledges that one of the strategies that they use to convince people to give Jesus control of their lives is the appropriation of alien, worldly culture in their fight to save souls. The connection that Bahamians of Haitian descent have with worldly (secular) culture in their lives at school, at their part-time jobs, and outside of church is a seemingly natural part of their lives rather than, to paraphrase Harding, an appropriation of alien, worldly culture. Unlike their parents, the members of the Victory Chapel *lajènes* who were born in the Bahamas are not necessarily trying to break with the secular world. Rather, they are incorporating aspects of the secular to reach the hearts and minds of other Bahamians of Haitian descent who have not yet accepted Christ and who, they believe, need to live as Christians, because of their legal status and the evils of the secular world such as drug use, fornication, and out-of-wedlock pregnancy.

But it is this very representation of self among Bahamians of Haitian descent that causes friction within the church and, by extension, in the

greater religious community. This is due to the cultural standards associated with the practice of Protestantism in Haiti that their parents try to
maintain while living in the Bahamas. Standards in dress and comportment are different in Haiti, and when the children of Haitian Protestants
are judged against Protestant religious culture developed in Haiti, many
devout Haitian Protestant migrants categorize them as *Pwotestan*. Therefore Bahamians of Haitian descent are in a difficult social position in the
Bahamas: They are in constant tension with a nation that rejects them,
as well as in generational and cultural tension with their parents and
churches. At the same time, they face difficulties trying to ascend from
their humble beginnings in a nation that blocks their social and political
integration. The performance of gospel songs like these, then, becomes a
way that *lajènes* members can envision a just and moral society, an even-
tual triumph over the societal forces that construct them as noncitizens.
Protestant Christianity, in the form of the Nazarene faith, is the starting
point where they try to reconcile the antagonistic forces that push their
social identities into a liminal space between Bahamian and Haitian.

Soldats de Christ et Haïtiens: Hymns and Nationalism at New Mission

Although not all Haitian Protestants intend to return to Haiti, they
all desire Haiti to become a stable nation-state. The desire to see Haiti
become a viable nation-state through Christ was expressed to me repeatedly by Haitian Protestants during my time in New Providence. This
sentiment was articulated also through the *adoration et louange* portion
of the Sunday morning service at New Haitian Mission Baptist Church.
One of my first observations about the services at New Mission was that
it was unlike the services at the Haitian Baptist churches I attended in
Port-au-Prince, Haiti, and the United States which were very reserved
and calm, as typical of *touloutoutou* churches. If there was one person
who called out or cried during service, that person would be the *predikatè* (the pastor or deliverer of the Lord's word for that day). The services

at New Mission, by contrast, lean toward a more charismatic style of worship (*tet mare*).

That morning, the pastor at New Mission continued with the reading of Psalm 96 ("Sing a New Song to the Lord"), selections from Chants d'espérance, more prayer, and a call for new visitors to introduce themselves. After the introductions, a deacon stood up on the stage and reminded the attendees that although we were in the Bahamas we should not forget Haiti. He then led the congregation in a rendition of "Soldats de Christ et Haïtiens [Soldiers of Christ and Haitians]," French hymn number 320 in the "Chants Nationaux Chretiens [National Christian Songs]" section of Chants d'espérance:

Soldats de Christ et Haïtiens,	Soldiers of Christ and Haitians,
Du ciel nous sommes citoyens.	We are citizens of heaven.
Dans la Parole du Seigneur,	In the word of God,
Nous trouvons le seul vrai bonheur.	We've found the only true happiness.
Refrain:	*Refrain:*
Sauve, Seigneur, bénis,	Save, O Lord, Bless,
Notre chère Haïti!	Our dear Haiti!
Petite nation,	Small nation,
Avance vers Sion,	Go forward to Zion,
A Dieu consacre-toi,	Consecrate yourself to God,
Fais de Jésus ton Roi.	Let Jesus be your King [your ruler].
Sauve, Seigneur,	Save, O Lord,
Bénis notre chère Haïti!	Bless our dear Haiti!
Soldats de Christ et Haïtiens,	Soldiers of Christ and Haitians,
Soyons unis à tous les siens,	Every one of us united,
Car dans le Testament Nouveau,	For in the New Testament,
Il nous a marqués de son sceau.	It has marked us with its stamp (the blood of Jesus).

Compatriotes Haïtiens,	Haitian Compatriots,
Du ciel devenez citoyens,	Become a citizen of heaven (the kingdom of God),
Chantez avec nous désormais:	Sing with us from now on:
Haïti pour Christ à jamais!	Haiti for Christ forever!

As ethnomusicologist Melvin Butler (2002) observes in his study of Haitian Pentecostal worship, the historical legacy of Haiti—including the combination of coup d'états, the violence against the masses of Haitians perpetrated by the Haitian military and Tonton Macoutes (a paramilitary force created by François Duvalier that terrorized the Haitian populace), and the countless American military interventions in the affairs of Haiti—has contributed to an ethos of militarism in Haitian culture. Aspects of this militarism can be seen in the lyrics of the hymn that was sung that morning at New Mission, equating citizenship in heaven with citizenship in Haiti ("Soldiers of Christ and Haitians, / We are citizens of heaven. / In the word of God, / We've found the only true happiness"). Instead of François Duvalier, Jean-Bertrand Aristide, or Michel Martelly as heads of the Haitian state, the refrain of the hymn declares "Consecrate yourself to God, / Let Jesus be your King [your ruler]." Ultimately, it is only through God that Haiti can be saved ("Save, O Lord, Bless our dear Haiti!"). That morning service was charged with emotion. People sang the hymn and you could hear some of their voices cracking. A church brother next to me could not finish the hymn and sat down with his head against his arm that was resting against the pew in front of him with a sad look etched across his face. A prayer for a resolution of the crisis in Haiti, which forced the Haitians at that church to live in the Bahamas, followed directly after the singing of the hymn.

The performance of "Soldats de Christ et Haïtiens" is representative of the Protestant faith but also reflects Haitian Protestant nationalism. That moment at New Mission went beyond a mere pride in their country, more than patriotism. The hymn was sung in February 2005, a year after

President Jean-Bertrand Aristide had been removed from office in a coup d'état, and five months after torrential rains had flooded Gonaïves, a city in Northern Haiti where many Haitian migrants in the Bahamas come from, leaving over two thousand people dead and over two hundred and fifty thousand people homeless. "Soldats de Christ et Haïtiens" took on a different meaning at a time where life in Haiti seemed to be getting worse. Within Haiti and its diaspora, the hymn is sung with the intent for a positive transformation in Haiti that only *Bondyè* can bring about.

The political expression that took place that morning at New Mission took the form of song and prayer. In both media the love of God was conflated with love for the nation (Haiti) as a way to find a solution to Haiti's crisis. Although none of the people assembled at New Mission that morning were physically in Haiti, their prayers and thoughts were directed toward their homeland. Whether they were living in the Bahamas with or without documentation, the day-to-day conditions they face make their prayers for change in Haiti pertinent so the kin they left behind can one day lead dignified lives in a nation transformed by the Holy Spirit.

Pastor Pierre and the Importance of a Christian Identity

Anthropologist Susan Harding (2000, 12) observes that preachers "convert the ancient recorded speech of the Bible once again into spoken language, translating it into local theological and cultural idioms and placing present events inside the sequence of Biblical stories." The pastors at International Tabernacle of Praise Ministries (Kevin Pierre), New Haitian Mission Baptist Church (Dr. Chérélus Exanté), and Victory Chapel Church of the Nazarene (Dr. Antoine Saint Louis) use biblical stories in their sermons to convince *moun ki poko konvèti* (the people who have not converted to Haitian Protestantism yet) to convert, provide instruction as to how to conduct oneself as a Christian, help adherents navigate the social terrain of the Bahamas and their diasporic religious community, and solve life's dilemmas while reflecting on the ideals of Haitian

Protestant culture. As these pastors interpret and translate biblical stories and verses through their sermons, they encourage migrants to be Christians as a solution to the problems that they face on a daily basis. Pastors Pierre, Saint Louis, and Exanté, whose churches provide a respite from a society where Haitians are exploited and oppressed, believe that leading the life of a Christian is the most effective tool that Haitians and Bahamians of Haitian descent can use to counter the prevailing stereotypes that Bahamians hold about Haitians (violent, savage, and disorganized), cope with discrimination in Bahamian society, and combat *move espri* (evil spirits), which are thought to prevent Haitians from leading a dignified life.

On April 25, 2005, I attended an evening service at International Tabernacle of Praise. By the time church started about ten people had assembled for a night of worship. The service took the format of the Sunday services I was accustomed to at New Mission and Victory Chapel: The church sang hymns from Chants d'espérance, such as number six from the Haitian Creole section (a direct translation of "Amazing Grace"). That night we read Psalm 39 from the New Testament. Pastor Pierre made some announcements including a call for prayer for the mother of a church member living in Haiti who was sick. After those announcements he introduced me to the congregation. After I made some brief comments about my Haitian genealogy, discussed my research in the Bahamas, and answered a few questions from the congregation, I sat down so that Pastor Pierre could preach.

Pastor Pierre preached from the book of Philippians 2.5–11, written by the apostle Paul, which deal with exaltation and Christ's humility:

Your attitude should be the same as that of Christ Jesus. Who, being in very nature God did not consider equality with God something to be grasped, but made himself nothing, taking the very nature of a servant, being made in human likeness. And being found in appearance as a man, he humbled himself and became obedient to death—even on a cross! Therefore God exalted him and gave him the name that is above every

name, that at the name of Jesus every knee should bow, in heaven and on
earth and under the earth, and every tongue confess that Jesus Christ is
Lord, to the glory of God the Father. (Ryrie Study Bible 1994, 1825)

According to Pastor Pierre, Paul, a biblical figure in the New Testament who would write letters from prison that became the book of
Philippians, accepted all things that came to him along the way in life
solely through the word of God. While preaching, Pastor Pierre would
ask the congregation at times, *"Ou ansanm ave m* [Are you with me]?"
to ensure that the congregation was paying attention and not sleeping,
like one older woman at the back of the church.

The most important point that Pastor Pierre made that night was that the
identity above all other identities for Haitians is a Christian identity, which
is a spiritual one, rather than a Haitian identity, which is both a national
and an ethnic identity. If the congregation was not living the word of God
and the life of a Christian, Pastor Pierre exhorted that evening, they would
not have eternal life in heaven. Pastor Pierre closed this sermon by telling
the congregation that Jesus is always with you, during good times and bad
times. Being a Christian from a Protestant denomination has implications
for the lives of Haitians in the Bahamas. Bahamians pride themselves as
being citizens of a Christian nation, where one can find most of the denominations associated with Christianity.[2] Some of the issues that Bahamians
debate are how to stem the tide of migration of Haitians to the Bahamas and
whether or not to grant amnesty to Haitians born and raised in the Bahamas (Bahamians of Haitian descent). As discussed earlier, Bahamians tend
to stereotype Haitians as violent, Vodou-worshipping savages who could
potentially disrupt the political stability of the Bahamas, and thus affect
the archipelagic nation's economy and way of life. So Haitians are seen as
a constant threat to the sovereignty and future of the nation. Some devout
Haitian Protestants hope that their identities as Christians may facilitate
integration and acceptance into a Christian Bahamas.

The Haitian Protestant belief that a Christian identity is more important than a Haitian identity also has meaning on an intra-ethnic (Haitian)

level. Pastor Pierre's sermon can be seen as a critique of how devout Haitian Protestant migrants view intra-Haitian interaction, especially in relation to Haitians who practice Vodou. Although he does not mention Vodou in his sermon, Vodou is an integral part of everyday Haitian life and it is his negative view of Vodou that helps Pastor Pierre organize his comments concerning the importance of a Christian identity for Haitians in the Bahamas. Because Haitian Protestants interpret Vodou as a backward way of life that promotes superstition and ignorance among Haitians, Protestant Christianity, to them, seems the only logical religious choice for any Haitian regardless of where they live in the world. Following the lessons taught in Haitian Protestant Sunday schools, attending Bible study, and prayer and maturity in one of the Haitian Protestant faiths leads to the formation of a Christian *karacktè* (character). This Christian *karacktè* is what Pastor Pierre sought to develop within his church for Haitians: a *karacktè* that informs migrants and their progeny regarding how to act in every potential social setting in which they find themselves while they reside in a foreign country that exploits and oppresses them.

Pastor Saint Louis and the Importance of Tithing

As part of International Tabernacle of Praise's first anniversary celebration, Pastor Pierre invited Bahamian and Haitian pastors in the community to preach on the theme of the two-week celebration called "One more year, Lord." Based on Luke 13.6–9 in the New Testament, the passage describes a parable Jesus once told to a crowd about a man who planted a fig tree in his vineyard, looked for fruit on the tree but found none. The man told the caretaker of the vineyard: "For three years now I've been coming to look for fruit on this fig tree and haven't found any. Cut it down! Why should it use up the soil?" The caretaker replied: "Sir, leave it alone for one more year, and I'll dig around it and fertilize it. If it bears fruit next year, fine! If not, then cut it down."[3] The Ryrie Study Bible notes that in this passage the fig tree is symbolic of the Jewish people and that God's judgment is sure, and that God's patience for his followers is great (1591). But the Haitian pastors who came to celebrate International Tabernacle of Praise's one-year anniversary interpreted this Bible passage through lenses that explained contemporary attitudes and issues facing Haitians living in the Bahamas.

On October 4, 2005, Dr. Saint Louis preached an animated sermon as part of International Tabernacle of Praise's anniversary celebration. That night he told Pastor Pierre's church, and the members of Victory Chapel who visited with him, that he knew why the nation of Haiti was in such a miserable state. His response did not look at the history of Haiti as a nation poorly inserted into the world economy. It did not mention the one hundred and fifty million gold francs Haiti had to pay France after the Haitian revolution, compromising Haiti's economic and infrastructural development to the present. There was no mention of the American Marine occupation of Haiti from 1915 to 1934, during which time the Haitian Constitution was rewritten for the benefit of foreign interests and an army was created that would be used against the Haitian people, pitting the Haitian state against the nation. Nor was there any mention of the Duvalier dictatorship—which lasted from 1957 to 1986 and expropriated millions of dollars of foreign aid earmarked for use to stem the endemic poverty in Haiti to support the Haitian military and François and Jean-Claude Duvalier's secret police, the Tonton Macoutes—or any other historical factors that have contributed to Haiti's current status as the poorest country in the Western Hemisphere. Instead, Pastor Saint Louis emphasized rules found in the Bible that a Christian should follow in order to be prosperous. He told all those who had convened in International Tabernacle of Praise that Haiti was such a poor country because Haitians who go to church do not tithe (that is, give 10 percent of their income to the church). Dr. Saint Louis would develop this spiritual strategy for renewing Haitians and Haiti in his sermon.

Dr. Saint Louis attested to the people in attendance that if International Tabernacle of Praise made it through its first year, it will make it to its second. He also encouraged the people to look ahead to the next year when times are hard, to see where they are going. In the parable in

Luke, the caretaker told the man who owned the vineyard that the fig tree would bear fruit. Pastor Saint Louis told us that night that in the future the tree would bear fruit just like Pastor Pierre's church would after time. In his sermon, he focused on the term *fondelai* (fertilizer) as a metaphor for what the church needed to grow. The *fondelai* for International Tabernacle of Praise was the time people gave to the church, the energy people used to keep it functioning, the talents people had that they could use for every function of the church, and finally, *trezò* (treasure, money). He would focus on tithing for the rest of his sermon.

Using verses from the New and Old Testaments, Pastor Saint Louis returned to the subject of tithing to explain the connection between the way Haitians in the Bahamas tithe and why Haiti is poor. Over the course of my time at all three churches, tithing was an issue that Pastors Pierre, Saint Louis, and Exanté stressed repeatedly in their sermons and the announcements they made to their respective churches, due to the reputation Haitians in this community had gained as poor tithers. Pastor Pierre admonished his congregation numerous times, for instance, that one way to receive blessings from God was through tithing the church properly. Pastor Exanté scolded New Mission's congregation before he delivered his sermon one morning when he told them that it was sinful for congregants to tithe their church back in Haiti but not to tithe his church, which protects and nourishes them in the Bahamas.

At International Tabernacle of Praise that night, Pastor Saint Louis explained through biblical examples that if a Haitian tithed properly, that blessings and money would flow into his or her life abundantly. He quoted Luke 6.38: "Give, and it will be given to you. A good measure, pressed down, shaken together and running over, will be poured into your lap. For with the measure you use, it will be measured to you" (Ryrie Study Bible 1994, 1575). This meant that for all of those Haitians who went to church on Sunday and only gave a dollar as an offering, they would only receive minimal blessings from God in return. Proverbs 3.9 reads, "Honor the Lord with your wealth, with the first fruits of all your crops" (Ryrie Study Bible 1994, 940). Pastor Saint Louis told the church: "When you give to

God last, you will receive last. When you give to God first, you'll receive first." If Protestants in Haiti tithed properly, he concluded, they would have enough money, food, and opportunities for Haitians to live in Haiti, meaning there would be no need for Haitians to come to the Bahamas.

In his sermon Pastor Saint Louis constructed a direct link between tithing and the future of Haiti. All three pastors—Pierre, Saint Louis, and Exanté—reasoned that instead of offering the church one dollar every Sunday, you should offer the church ten or twenty dollars. Then you, as a Haitian Protestant who migrated to the Bahamas with hopes of a better life, would see that things would get better in your life, that blessings would fall down from heaven. For example, you might receive a raise at your job. Your request for permanent residence in the Bahamas might be granted. Your child who was born in the Bahamas might be granted citizenship. You might finally make it to the United States. In other words, proper tithing, meaning following God's edict to tithe 10 percent of one's income, would lead to a direct, material improvement in the life of a Haitian Protestant.

What was striking about Pastor Saint Louis's sermon was that he connected the fate of Haiti to tithing and the Haitian individual. The only way that Haiti could change from a disgraced and poor nation to a nation where prosperity and peace reigned—a nation that would be recognized as an equal member among nations around the world—was through tithing. Haiti's salvation would not occur through the cancellation of debt repayment or the repayment of the one hundred and fifty million gold Francs that France had requested in the nineteenth century. Like Pastor Pierre's sermon, Pastor Saint Louis's sermon linked the practice of tithing to the cultivation of an overall Protestant Christian identity for Haitians, an identity lacking among Haitians in the Bahamas but crucial, in both of their opinions, to the reversal of misfortune among Haitians generally.

Pastor Exanté and Being Christian

New Mission also participated in International Tabernacle of Praise's weeklong anniversary celebration through a sermon delivered to both congregations by Pastor Exanté. Pastor Exanté preached from Luke 13.6–9 in the New Testament, the same Bible passage that Pastor Saint Louis referred to in his sermon. He told the congregation that night that there were spiritual and moral lessons in this biblical passage, but that one must look at other Bible verses to understand those verses and International Tabernacle of Praise's theme of "One more year, Lord." Dr. Exanté noted that Christians should consult the book of Matthew 21.18–22 to understand the meaning of International Tabernacle of Praise's anniversary theme:

> Early in the morning, as he was on his way back to the city, [Jesus] was hungry. Seeing a fig tree by the road, he went up to it but found nothing on it except leaves. Then he said to it, "May you never bear fruit again!" Immediately the tree withered. When the disciples saw this, they were amazed. "How did the fig tree wither so quickly?" they asked. Jesus replied, "I tell you the truth, if you have faith and do not doubt, not only can you do what was done to the fig tree, but also you can say to this mountain, 'Go, throw yourself into the sea,' and it will be done. If you believe, you will receive whatever you ask for in prayer." (Ryrie Study Bible 1994, 1498)

Like the passage from Luke, the fig tree in the book of Matthew was used again as a symbol of how a *Kretyen* should believe and follow the teachings of Jesus Christ and God, lest that person become like the withered fig tree in the parable. After reading the passage, Pastor Exanté posed this question to the congregation: "What have you produced for the Lord since you accepted Christ?" The question garnered a positive reaction of shouts of "Amen" and "Hallelujah" from the mixed assembly of adherents from International Tabernacle of Praise and New Mission. He continued: "We are supposed to use our talents for the church. You are a tree and you are supposed to bear fruit."

Pastor Exanté then focused the congregation's attention again on the theme of "One more year, Lord" by citing Luke 13.8, which reads: "'Sir,' the man replied, 'leave it alone for one more year, and I'll dig around it and fertilize it'" (Ryrie Study Bible 1994, 1591). According to Dr. Exanté, the gardener interceded on behalf of the tree to give it one more year to bear fruit. Dr. Exanté then told his congregation that to understand who the gardener is that we must look to John 15, where Jesus, the Son of God says:

> I am the true vine, and my Father [God] is the gardener. He cuts off every branch in me that bears no fruit, while every branch that does bear fruit he prunes so that it will be even more fruitful. You are already clean because of the word I have spoken to you. Remain in me, and I will remain in you. No branch can bear fruit by itself; it must remain in the vine. Neither can you bear fruit unless you remain in me. (Ryrie Study Bible 1994, 1649)

This decree spoken by Jesus instructs Christians to continue to believe and do the work of God (leading a Christian life, spreading the word of God) lest they stop bearing fruit. Revealing to the attendees that God was the gardener, Dr. Exanté directed the people present that night to Romans 2.4: "Or do you show contempt for the riches of his kindness, tolerance and patience, not realizing that God's kindness leads you toward repentance?" (Ryrie Study Bible 1994, 1728). It is through the gardener's (God's) kindness, tolerance, and patience that Haitians remain in the Bahamas, Pastor Exanté remarked, and it is the gardener's patience that allows Haitians to have one more year. At this point he shouted out: "I will give myself to the Lord and I will repent!" He wanted to exhort all of the people who were present that night: those who had not converted yet, those who were backsliding and needed to rededicate themselves to the Lord, and those who were maturing in the Protestant Christian faith. Some of the members of International Tabernacle of Praise made their way to the front of the church and stood by the pulpit because of how the sermon resonated with them.

Dr. Exanté used one more Bible verse to illustrate the seriousness of each person's mortality from 2 Peter 3.17–18: "Therefore, dear friends, since you already know this, be on your guard so that you may not be

carried away by the error of lawless men and fall from your secure position. But grow in the grace and knowledge of our Lord and Savior Jesus
Christ. To him be the glory both now and forever! Amen" (Ryrie Study
Bible 1994, 1923). He concluded his sermon by reminding everyone that
people should use the education, knowledge and talents that they developed in Haiti for the Lord because they never know when they will die.
They may not get another chance to do so, because death and eternity in
hell are the consequence for disobeying the gardener. Pastor Pierre began
to sing a hymn encouraging those who had not converted yet to do so
but no one came up to the pulpit for prayer or conversion.

As noted in the Ryrie Study Bible (1994, 1923) about the last passage
Pastor Exanté referenced, "bear in mind" means to understand that the
delay of the return of the Lord is intended as an opportunity for humans
to be saved. After living in the Bahamas for more than twenty-five years,
Pastor Exanté knew that there were some people who attended the Haitian Protestant churches of New Providence to edify their souls and
continue their maturation as Christians. There were other Haitians who
never heard of, or paid attention to, the Protestant gospel of Jesus Christ
while they were in Haiti. Many of them only attended Haitian Protestant
churches because the church was one of the few institutions in Bahamian
society that addressed their social needs. Some Haitians go to church to
find a job. Others go to church with the sole intent to find a partner who
may later become their common-law spouse in the Bahamas. Still others
go to Haitian Protestant churches to socialize with their friends during
Sunday school and services, and after church.

Based on the unwritten rules of appearance and comportment of Protestant Christianity in Haiti, many migrants have inappropriate hairstyles
and wear inappropriate clothing, makeup, and jewelry at church and
dress and carry themselves inappropriately outside of church. Pastor
Exanté's sermon, then, was also directed at those who attend Haitian
Protestant churches for all the reasons except the most important ones: to
worship *Bondyè*, tithe God's church, and grow in their faith as Christians.
On more than one occasion at New Mission, Pastor Exanté acknowledged

that not everyone who goes to church is saved or baptized. Furthermore, those who did not know the security that Jesus Christ provides to those who believe in Him would perish with the promise of a hellish afterlife that Protestant Christianity guarantees. At the same time, Pastor Exanté was also preaching to the baptized members of churches who considered themselves to be Christians but had slid back into the lives that defined them as sinners: gambling, drinking, prostitution, wearing inappropriate clothes in and out of church, and attending Vodou consults and cockfights—activities strictly forbidden by the ascetic religious culture associated with Protestant Christianity in Haiti. He warned this group of backsliders and protesters that they should be worried about their salvation and that the solution is to combat life's challenges through a strong Christian identity that bears fruit for the church and for oneself, as well as for the nation of Haiti.

Chapter 5 looks more closely at the three symbolic boundaries—*Kretyen*, *Pwotestan*, and *moun ki poko konvèti*—to help explain how devout migrants in New Providence develop a general sense of organization and order within their diasporic religious community, how they critique their community and community members, and what they consider to be missing from individuals and from Haiti.

5

"The People Who Have Not Converted Yet," Protestant, and Christian

On December 10, 2005, Dieunous Senatus, assistant pastor of Victory Chapel Church of the Nazarene, buried his wife. She had passed away as a result of preeclampsia, a rapidly progressive medical condition in pregnant women characterized by high blood pressure and the presence of protein in the mother's urine. Swelling, sudden weight gain, headaches, and changes in vision are important symptoms.[1] The only cure for preeclampsia is through the delivery of the baby. In her case, she reached the hospital, had seizures, and died in childbirth.

Pastor Senatus attended the Sunday evening service after the funeral with one of his wife's sisters, who wanted to sing a song in her deceased sister's honor. The sister prefaced her impending performance with an announcement that was made by a deacon who was directing the service that evening. The sister did not have a dress to wear for that evening's service and was worried about coming to church wearing pants. The deacon told the congregation that her not having the proper clothes to wear should not prevent her from coming to sing and worship at Mrs. Senatus's church.[2] Under normal circumstances, she probably would not have been allowed to sing in church because of her inappropriate clothing. After the announcement, however, the congregation agreed that it would be fine for her to perform the tribute song.

As this anecdote demonstrates, there are appropriate and inappropriate ways of dressing and comporting oneself in this religious community. The observations of devout Haitian Protestant migrants about the *konpòtman* (comportment, behavior) and *aparans* (appearance, dress) of other Haitian migrants enable them to draw the boundaries of *Kreyten* and the closely related moral boundaries of *Pwotestan* and *moun ki poko konvèti*. The key factor that identifies a person as *Kretyen* is a *krent pou Bondyè* (fear of God) that controls one's appearance and comportment.

Moun Ki Poko Konvèti

To understand Haitian Protestantism comprehensively, it is important to view it as an attempt to maintain and sustain a way of life that is set apart from the trappings of a secular world filled with evil spirits and sinful temptations. This secular world is antithetical to a devout existence and can only be reconciled through the conversion of *moun ki poko konvèti*—that is, other Haitians who neither practice nor have converted to some form of Protestant Christianity. The people who fall into the *moun ki poko konvèti* category can include Bahamians, Haitians who practice Vodou, and Bahamians of Haitian descent, but mostly those whom devout Haitian Protestant migrants refer to as Haitian Catholics.

Although some of my research consultants considered certain Catholics good Christians, the majority of those I interviewed considered them to be morally corrupt. They viewed Catholics as people one would most likely find drinking, smoking, and swearing in public. They also believe that a married Catholic is likely involved in extramarital affairs; behavior that is strictly forbidden in the Old and New Testaments. Views about the immorality of Catholics also extend to perceptions of their everyday appearance. According to my research consultants, Haitian Catholic women wear tight clothes, low V-neck blouses, makeup, rings, necklaces, and earrings. Haitian Catholic men have long hair, unkempt Afros, dreadlocks, and cornrows, and wear wrinkled and baggy clothes, earrings, and chains.[3] Thus, "the people who have not converted yet" resemble secular Haitians. While this caricature of Catholics may seem harsh, devout Haitian Protestant migrants construct their religious identities primarily in opposition to this perception. For these migrants, it is important that they do not invite comparison to the comportment, dress, or hairstyles of a group that, to them, symbolizes sin. The emphasis that devout Haitian Protestant migrants in New Providence place on a person's behavior and appearance reflects the rules of Protestant Christian religious culture in Haiti.[4]

Konpòtman

As we have seen, devout Haitian Protestant migrants often view being *Kretyen* (Christian) and being *Pwotestan* (Protestant) as two separate yet related identities. A *Pwotestan* is someone who knows how to perform certain aspects of Haitian Protestant culture well when attending services. The person is familiar with the usual hymns and responds with shouts of "*Alelouya* [Hallelujah]," "*Beniswa Letènel* [Praise the Lord]," and "Amen" at appropriate times during fiery sermons. However, if that same person drinks rum and places bets at local cockfights in his private life after church, then that person is sinning without remorse and is therefore not viewed as a Christian. In the eyes of devout Haitian Protestants, that person exhibits no observable spiritual transformation that would demonstrate a dedication to God and a Christian way of being as is the case with a *Kretyen*.

One of the ways devout Haitian Protestant migrants determine whether a person is a *Pwotestan* or a *Kretyen* is by observing the person's *konpòtman* (comportment). Brother Jonas, who attended New Haitian Mission Baptist Church, elucidated this for me. Twenty-three years old at the time of our interview, Brother Jonas identified himself as Protestant and Baptist. Like the majority of Haitian transmigrants in the Bahamas, he grew up in Haiti's Northwestern department. He accepted Christ as his personal savior at an early age in a village outside of Bassin Bleu and attended Baptist church intermittently for most of his life but, due to Haiti's socioeconomic crisis, became more serious about his faith at age twenty. Because of high unemployment and limited funds to continue his education, he migrated to the Bahamas. At *lajènes* meetings, Jonas would regale the audience with original raps, songs, and impromptu sermons about what a Christian needed to do to stay on the right path to heaven.

He explained that his faith in God became stronger after his arrival in New Providence and that there was a difference between Haitian Protestants in New Providence and Protestant Christians in Haiti:

> Sometimes where you are, you find that not every person has the same comportment. So, there are people . . . who have good comportment: the way that they talk, the way they dress, the way they function. That's very good but you'll find people [at the church and in the Haitian Protestant community] who don't act the same way but since that person is being exposed to the Gospel [of Jesus Christ], the person has the opportunity to change. . . . I mostly see that there's some work that some people need to do, maybe in how they function, their ways, so they can have that change in their lives.[5]

In his comments Brother Jonas indicates that the way that people comport themselves and dress are intimately tied to who they are as Christians. This understanding of how a Christian is supposed to exist in the world was shaped by his or her religious experiences in Haiti. When Brother Jonas encounters a Haitian Protestant migrant who talks, dresses, or behaves in ways that are contradictory to biblical teachings and the culture of Haitian Protestantism, he tends not to view that person as a Christian. It is the Gospel of Jesus Christ—and one's adherence to the Gospel through proper comportment, dress, and a *krent pou Bondyè*—that transforms a migrant into a devout Christian.[6]

Brother Jonas also articulated a theme that I heard in later conversations and interviews: that something is wrong with the Haitian Protestant community of New Providence. His opinion of the migrant Protestant community focused on *plasaj* (common-law marriage), the most frequent example of sinful behavior used by my research consultants:

> Okay, it's . . . everything is here . . . but [the community] doesn't function properly. How can I explain to you that everything is here, but it doesn't function properly? There are things that the Bible *says* [his emphasis];

everything is there [the rules that a Christian is supposed to follow and abide by]. But there are people who use logic. How so? There are people who [come to the Bahamas,] let's say this person is a woman. She doesn't have her mother, she doesn't have her father, but she simply finds a man who picks her up, who pays for a room in a house for her, without being married, and . . . now they're living [together.] And this person says she's doing this because of her situation. She must do it. But the Bible doesn't give us this kind of logic. The Bible specifically says if [a man and a woman] live together, they are supposed to be married. You're married and you are living together. That's what the Bible explains. . . .

If this person says to God, "Savior, I've entered this country. I've entered this country because of an economic situation and this is not the country I was born in. I ask you, please I do not want to do things that are *bad* [his emphasis]. I don't want [to] carry myself in a manner that I shouldn't, in a way the Bible says I shouldn't carry myself. I want to carry myself in a way that You [God] want me to carry myself, the way You explained I should carry myself according to the Bible. I ask You for a chance. Give me an opportunity to respect the Bible. I respect what You told me. I respect your Word so I don't commit acts against Your word."[7]

Common-law marriage—a union between a man and a woman recognized by public opinion but not by law (Métraux 1959, 377)—is common in Haiti's Northwestern department. In fact, many of my research consultants referred to themselves as *pitit deyò*, meaning that they were born from unions such as these. Because of laws that limit educational and employment opportunities for undocumented men and women in the Bahamas, *plasaj* is a familiar and logical living arrangement.[8]

But *plasaj* is sinful according to the Protestant Christian community of Haiti and devout Haitian Protestant migrants in the Bahamas. When a Haitian accepts Christ as his or her personal savior, the Protestant community expects the convert to break sinful habits. This means that there are places now that converts cannot go to anymore, there are acts that they are not supposed to commit anymore, and there are people with whom they are not supposed to associate anymore. *Plasaj* can only be rectified through repentance and marriage. The belief in heterosexual marriage is already understood and reinforced through adult Sunday school lessons from Protestant Christian education manuals imported from Haiti, through sermons from evangelists and pastors, and through Bible study and baptism classes.

By criticizing other members of his religious community who engage in *plasaj*, Brother Jonas constructs himself as distinct from fellow church members, and as someone who is morally superior to those who participate in common-law marriages. But it is not only his condemnation of their choices that makes him different from his "sinful" church members. Brother Jonas also discussed how a Christian is supposed to live:

> Here you find there are people who are living, the place where they're living, with a person who is not living in the Gospel. When this person comes [to the Bahamas,] it's this person who falls along the way, but this person is not carrying himself/herself according to the Gospel. And then, that gives a person the opportunity not to go to church. You don't find this chance. Why so? Because of the place the person is living in. [S/]He has no way to get to church. [S/]He isn't hearing the message [of God]. [S/]He's not hearing the Word. [S/]He falls into a group of people who never go to church. This allows his[/her] mind to weaken and allows him[/her] to fall into the same condition of the other people around him[/her].
>
> For me, personally, I'm praying that I'm always speaking to God, I'm asking for a chance for my other brothers and sisters [in Christ]. I'm always asking for a chance. Remember those who don't have anyone because that's part of the problem. When you don't have anyone [like family], you can always fall into any place. You can fall into things and get stuck there because you don't have other people to get you out of those situations. But for me anyway God has something He can do in a situation.[9]

Brother Jonas constructs himself as Christian first when he condemns *plasaj* as a sin and in his continuing critique of how a Christian is supposed to live. He believes that to be Christian you must obey God's word even though *plasaj* might, for example, make a young woman's life in a foreign country easier by having a man help support the common-law household they would create. Brother Jonas also believes that a Christian should pray for others with the hope that God will help those who are less fortunate than them and who are living in sin. This belief that God will rectify everything, that God will guide people in making the right decisions for their lives, and that God will take care of people no matter what their situation, is a fundamental difference between *Kretyens* and *Pwotestans* in this community.

Aparans

Within Protestant communities in Haiti the *aparans* (appearance) of church members is an important identity marker that Haitian adherents, regardless of their denominational affiliation, use to police the borders they create to maintain their religious identities. Carbon copies of rules about Haitian missionary dress codes, denominational beliefs about acceptable clothing, and biblical teachings referencing attire are circulated within Haitian Protestant culture. Combined, they help to create a religious culture where appearance reflects piety.

In the devout Protestant community of Haiti, women tend to be plain in appearance. Pentecostal women, for example, do not wear makeup or jewelry but blouses and skirts or dresses with sensible shoes (flats and low heels). Men tend not to wear their hair long but very short or in a short, neat Afro. Men also wear ties with long-sleeved collared shirts, suits, long dress pants, and short-sleeved, collared shirts. This dress code for women and men is not just for church on Sundays but carries over to weekly church activities, such as Bible study and prayer services, and to their workplaces. It represents civility, character, religious devotion, and the adherents' faith everywhere they go in Haiti. Haitian Protestant fashion is a symbolic representation of a true transformation of the souls of Haitians. It is antithetical to Vodou, a way of life that, according to devout Haitian Protestants, attracts evil spirits and is partly responsible for Haiti's endemic poverty and governmental corruption.

Haitian Protestants partly developed and reinforced their culture of appearance through fundamentalist interpretations of biblical passages referring to appearance. First Corinthians 11 contains the Apostle Paul's instructions for public worship and how men and women should appear when worshipping God. First Corinthians 11.5 states, "And every woman who prays or prophesies with her head uncovered dishonors her head—it is just as though her head were shaved."[10] First Corinthians 11.14 refers to men and their appearance: "Does not the very nature of things teach you that if a man has long hair, it is a disgrace to him?"[11] Additional appearance references are also found in the first book of Timothy, also written by the Apostle Paul. First Timothy 2.9–10 gives the following instructions: "I also want women to dress modestly, with decency and propriety, not with braided hair or gold or pearls or expensive clothes, but with good deeds, appropriate for women who profess to worship God."[12]

Appearance continues to be important to devout Haitian Protestant migrants in the Bahamas and is a key determinant in their observations of who is *Kretyen* and who is not. This view is apparent in the comments of Sister Maude, a member of International Tabernacle of Praise whom I introduced earlier. Her comments reveal the difficulty she encountered when attempting to distinguish Christians from "the people who have not converted yet." Her comments also describe what a *Pwotestan* (someone who resembles *moun ki poko konvèti*) can look like and how that person behaves by focusing her observations on the appearance of women at Haitian Protestant churches in New Providence:

If the person doesn't tell you that they are a Christian, you cannot tell if they are a Christian. Because this person carries him- or herself the same way everyone else does, like all the people who haven't converted yet. This person is walking, for example, a woman. She puts fake hair in her head [wears a wig or extensions]. She's wearing makeup. She does her eyebrows. They scratch the back of their heads like people who haven't accepted

Christ yet. She has fifty holes in her ears [for earrings], and wears a bunch of earrings, rings, chains, and things like that. These are things for people who haven't converted yet.

People in church [in New Providence] are like that, too. And then this same person is involved in all of the activities of the church. She's singing in the chorus, she's involved in everything at the church, and she looks like a Jezebel![13]

Sister Maude's comments about the Haitian Protestant migrant community reflected her irritation with the behavior and appearance of other churchgoers. Her comment about people who "scratch the back of their heads like people who haven't accepted Christ yet" is a reference to those women who wear wigs, weaves, and braids in their hair and scratch their heads when their scalps are itchy. Overall, Sister Maude deemed the diasporic religious community to be in complete disorder:

You see a person. He or she is in a common-law marriage [*plasaj*].[14] And this person is doing everything in the church. This person is involved in all of the church activities. I haven't seen that at my church back in Haiti. The person is married and has a girlfriend or has a boyfriend. This person is participating in all of the church activities. [The church] doesn't sanction the person. They don't say anything. It's like the community is in complete disorder. It lacks true seriousness.

The pastor doesn't say anything about it. So I don't see any differences between the Protestant churches of New Providence. For example, when you are a Christian you don't need to open your mouth to tell someone that you're a Christian, you understand what I'm saying? You don't need to open your mouth and tell people this when you arrive some place: "I'm a Christian. I go to such and such's church in New Providence . . .

At my home church in Haiti . . . they're more Christian in Haiti. It's more Christian in Haiti. They don't have to go around announcing that they are Christian. When you are in front of a person, you can see that that person is a Christian, you understand?

Because you can see the difference in the person. You see the difference in the person.[15]

At this point in our conversation, I interjected, "you see a difference in the person, in their appearance and their comportment" which got her excited:

Yes! Women in Nassau wear tight pants and short skirts. They can't even sit. They can't even bend [because their clothes are so tight]. Haiti doesn't have that. A person . . . for example let's take my home church. If a young woman wears pants and if she sees me coming as a person in her church, she'll go and hide. She won't let you see her. She won't let you see her because she knows if you see her, you'll go tell the church, and then she'll be sanctioned. She won't let you see her. Here [in the Bahamas], they don't check for these kinds of things.[16]

Protestant Christianity as it is practiced in Haiti is the referent that organizes Sister Maude's critique and helps her to construct Haitians within this diasporic religious community as *Pwotestan*. Based on her observations, some Haitian Protestant migrants generally do not look like or behave like Protestant Christians in Haiti, suggesting that they are not truly Christians. The behavior and appearance of devout Protestant Christians are supposed to reflect an inner transformation that begins when they converted and continues on the path to becoming a Christian through maturity in knowledge of the Gospel of Jesus Christ, religious activities, and adult baptism. It is easier for Sister Maude to identify who is truly *Kretyen* in Haiti than it is for her to identify who is *Kretyen* in the Bahamas. This is because of the way devout adherents in Haiti dress and comport themselves, as compared to how some Haitian Protestant migrants dress and comport themselves in New Providence. It is difficult and troubling for Sister Maude to accept those people who identify themselves as Christian but look and comport themselves like *moun ki poko konvèti* within the confines of their church in the Bahamas.

Sister Maude's example of a young woman wearing pants who, when seen by a member of her church, runs and hides for fear of church sanction is consistent with sociologist Max Weber's (1946, 314–316) assertion that Protestant church congregations in the United States at the turn of the twentieth century were self-governing and extraordinarily self-disciplined. In Weber's discussion on the importance of communion (*lasentsen*) among the independents and Baptists, there was a struggle against the domination of the congregation by theologians. The struggle led to what Weber called the clericalization of the lay members. This meant that they took over the functions of moral control "through self-government, admonition, and possible excommunication" (317). Clericalization, specifically the issues of self-government and admonition, is an important aspect of the culture of Protestantism in Haiti that some devout Haitian Protestant migrants are familiar with and try to implement in the Bahamas. Sister Maude's comments demonstrate that the features of self-government and admonition, prevalent at her church in Haiti, are missing at her New Providence church and from Haitian Protestant Christian life in the Bahamas. Furthermore, many Haitian Protestant migrants, in Sister Maude's opinion, are not devout and are ignoring the principles, ideals, and beliefs developed in Haiti. Through her critique, Sister Maude also constructs herself as a *Kretyen*.

Kretyen

As mentioned earlier, Brother Jonas was troubled by the way Haitian Protestant migrants comported themselves. Sister Maude believed that the migrant community of Haitian Protestants was in complete disorder. These comments illuminate a lingering dissatisfaction with the Haitian Protestant migrant community of New Providence among some devout Haitian Protestants. But the subtexts of their comments also allude to the dimensions of what it means to be a *Kretyen*. Sister Maude averred that you can "see a difference in the person" when they are *Kretyen*. But aside from these outward indexes of behavior and appearance, there is another factor that helps some Haitian Protestants in New Providence to distinguish a *Pwotestan* from a *Kretyen—krent pou Bondyè*, a fear of God. Brother Nicholas, a New Mission church member, explained this concept to me.

Brother Nicholas never consciously accepted Christ while living in Haiti. He does remember being baptized at his first church in Jacmel in 1988. When he moved to Port-au-Prince, he rededicated himself to the Lord after some backsliding. At the time of our interview, he was thirty-four years old and had the goal of immigrating to the United States one day so that he could either work as an auto mechanic or continue studying accounting. During his time in New Providence, he depended on the church for his social and spiritual needs. Like Sister Maude, Brother Nicholas was part of a growing number of Haitians in the Bahamas who migrated from Port-au-Prince. After visiting Pentecostal and Nazarene churches during his first few weeks in the Bahamas, he decided on New Haitian Mission Baptist Church, where he appreciated the different weekly church activities, guest pastors from abroad, and the church seminary. New Mission, in his estimation, helped him to grow intellectually and spiritually.

During our interview, Brother Nicholas admitted that it was difficult at times to discern who was a *Kretyen* and who was a *Pwotestan*:

When you hear people saying "Protestant," that's a person who is protesting or arguing against something. Sometimes when you don't come to church you can call that person "Protestant," you don't like something, you don't like it, you argue against it. But they still use that language, especially in our country [Haiti], to mean that the Protestant can go to church. Like the person goes to a church that is not Catholic, understand? S/He left the Catholic religion and then they are Protestant, understand? This means that everyone should not be involved in the Catholic religion. And then the person comes to church, s/he is Protestant. Everyone who is in the church, we are all Protestant whereas, he can, while they are [in the Bahamas,] he has a wife in Haiti and while he is [in the Bahamas,] he has another wife. But he is inside the church. In Haiti that is a Protestant. It could be a young woman [who left her boyfriend in Haiti] or young man who left his girlfriend . . . and while he is [in the Bahamas,] he has a woman who is pregnant with his child. He has ten women pregnant while he is in church. That is a Protestant.[17]

Brother Nicholas broadens our knowledge about what a Protestant is. A Protestant is an adherent of some form of Protestant Christianity. A *Pwotestan* is also a person who protests something, like Haitian Catholicism, yet lacks a transformation and reorientation to Haitian Protestant Christian culture. Brother Nicholas suggests that when people leave Catholicism in protest, they instantly become Protestants. But all they are doing, in his opinion, is protesting Catholicism because there has been no change in their behavior. Brother Nicholas makes this clear in his exaggerated example of the Protestant man who has a wife in Haiti and has also impregnated ten women in the Bahamas. He also suggests that the symbolic boundary of *Pwotestan* is understood in Haiti as a person who is a churchgoer and sinner and has not had a religious or behavioral transformation yet.

Brother Nicholas also offers other examples of differences between a *Kretyen* and a *Pwotestan*:

But [for] a person who is a Christian, everything is fine. Moreover, a Christian is a person who is waiting for the return of Jesus Christ. This means there are a bunch of things *you cannot do* [his emphasis], understand? There are [a] bunch of things that you cannot do. A *Kretyen* is a person who is regenerated. A *Kretyen* is someone who is reborn. And there are a bunch of things you cannot do. You know the principles of the Holy Bible. That person does not accept everything. But when s/he feels that they want something, you have a need, you have a necessity, you cannot do those [sinful] things [that you want to do]. Pray to God to help you. If your wife is never here or your husband is not beside you, they are in Haiti, you'll pray [to] God to help you find a way for your husband [to come to the Bahamas] or find a way to get your wife [to come to the Bahamas,] or you yourself you go back to your wife or your husband, understand?

You cannot start a relationship with another woman even if you feel the need [to], you understand? Because a person who is Christian . . . you do something that is not good, understand? And then you feel your conscience reproach you, understand? Because you are guilty. You did something that was not good. But everything that you do, at the same time it's not good, you're an adulterer, you killed someone in a robbery and your conscience has never reproached you? That means you're not truly Christian. You go to church too but you're not a Christian. So there's a difference between a person who is Christian and a person who is a Protestant.[18]

Brother Nicholas shares the same beliefs of previous critics of Haitian Protestantism in the Bahamas when he observes that there are things that a Christian cannot do. The main difference between his critique and the critiques of his predecessors is his mention of conscience. Someone who possesses a Protestant Christian conscience is supposed to regret the sins that he or she has committed. Christians are supposed to pray to God for a positive change to their circumstances and to extinguish their sinful desires. Those people who are in church and who commit grave sins are not Christians in Brother Nicholas's estimation because there is no guilt or remorse for the egregious sins that they have committed.

In the course of the interview, I asked if a *Pwotestan* had a fear of God: "I will not say that they both have a fear of God because the fear is different. Because *it is the fear of God that causes you not to do things that you're not supposed to do* [my emphasis]. Like a Christian has the fear of God [inside of himself/herself]. The Protestant knows that God exists, understand? S/He does not have what is called 'the fear of God' in his or her home."[19] I then asked Brother Nicholas if Protestants could practice Vodou, a view commonly held by Bahamians and others who believe that Haitian conversions to evangelical forms of Protestantism are rarely about a genuine religious transformation or a radical reorientation of religious beliefs. He responded:

Yes. There are a lot of Protestants [practicing Vodou]. For example, there are people [who practice Vodou] while they are [in Nassau] and then those same people are in church. They [come] to church normally but then if they have a headache, [they] will leave. If [they] sprain something..., if [they have] an accident..., or if [they] fall down [and hurt themselves]..., now in their spirit they think that it was *dyab* [the Devil] who was trying to harm them or someone in their family. Now that same person sends some money to Haiti, sends the money for his/her mother or father to go see what is happening. [This means that they] go to the Vodou priest's house on his/her behalf.[20]

Brother Nicholas argues that a *Pwotestan* is missing a *krent pou Bondyè*, though he concedes that Protestants know that God exists. Christians' fear of God is what causes them not to do things that are considered sinful and taboo according to their interpretation of biblical passages and religious culture. The act of consultation with Vodou priests and priestesses in Brother Nicholas's story demonstrates that he believes that those who are *Pwotestan* have not reoriented their worldview according to the tenets, principles, and culture of Haitian Protestantism. The use of an *oungan* (Vodou priest) by Protestants shows that they believe in other supernatural forces in the world, not in the supreme power of *Jezu* (Jesus).[21]

As anthropologist Alfred Métraux (1959, 352) observes in his ethnography of Vodou in Haiti, many *vodouizan* (Vodou practitioners) also convert to Protestant forms of Christianity not because Vodou failed to supply their need for a purer, loftier religion, but on the contrary, because they felt themselves to be the target of angry *lwa* and sought refuge in Protestantism. Anthropologist Karen Richman (2005) discusses this aspect of Haitian Protestantism in her work concerning Vodou and migration and provides another explanation of why *moun ki poko konvèti* convert to Protestant forms of Christianity: protesting ritual exploitation that occurs in the transnational practice of Vodou. The main protagonist in Richman's ethnography was named Ti Chini (Little Caterpillar), a Haitian migrant who worked as a day laborer in South Florida to support his family in Ti Rivye, Haiti. Ti Chini practiced Vodou transnationally through cassettes that he sent to his village in Haiti and the cassettes his family in Haiti would send back to him.

After visiting his family and ancestral spirits (*lwa*) in Haiti in 1988, Ti Chini returned to Florida to work in the orange fields of Fort Pierce. Without his knowledge one of his brothers in Ti Rivye who was sick and needed money appropriated Ti Chini's investments including a business he started called *fe sinema* (making cinema, showing movies in a house and charging people for the movies). Around this time Ti Chini fell from a ladder while picking oranges and had to have an operation on his shoulder. It was then that his doctors informed him of the onset of diabetes. Getting by on gifts and loans for the next year until his court case against his employer was settled for ten thousand dollars, Ti Chini called Karen to inform her of his conversion to a Protestant religion. She was stunned because as she notes: "Protestant conversion would have required absolute disavowal of relations with *lwa* and ancestors (as well as a break with Catholicism). It would have meant relinquishment of Caterpillar's cast ritual knowledge and talent, and of his expected accession to the position of *gangan* (Vodou priest, male shaman) of the House" (Richman 2005, 251). Ti Chini explained in a recorded letter to Karen:

> Well, Karen, here is the reason why I converted. Regardless, I would have converted anyway. How could I be serving *lwa* for all of these problems to keep on happening to me in both the land of Miami and in the land of Haiti? Why? When a *lwa* needs to eat, I provide for him/her. If I'm [sitting] over here working these lousy jobs, and *Se Byen* [his older brother] sends word that he's going to do such and such work in Haiti, like it or not, I have to send off $200 or $300. Why? For the *lwa*. And then, after I've done all that work, who should have the biggest problems but me. (252)

In her analysis of Ti Chini's cassette letter Richman rightly points out that he did not convert to Protestantism until conversion presented the ultimate personal weapon for resisting the ritual system that symbolically exploited him as a source of support for his kin in Haiti. Furthermore, Ti Chini's commentary reveals that his conversion was not due to a "sudden, deep faith in a new, better religion" but was in fact resistance to ritual exploitation (258–259).

Brother Nicholas also provided an example from his own life about a coworker in the Bahamas that illustrated the differences between a *Kretyen* and a *Pwotestan*:

> But a Christian won't ever do this because he/she doesn't believe [in Vodou] . . . let me give you an example that's simple. There is a young man where I work and while he was working at the job, he fell. He was climbing a coconut tree he was cleaning, a palm tree. He fell and he said that it was someone who made him fall, understand? It was something that happened. After that he contacted someone in his family back in Haiti about this. And then his family member went and made a request for him to find out if it was or was not someone trying to hurt him. I do not know what his family said [about this. Whether or not a Vodou priest or priestess believed someone was trying to hurt the young man].
>
> The young man went to Haiti after this happened. When he went [to Haiti], he went and got something, understand? Something to protect him [an amulet], protection, from his home in Haiti. This young man now believes that nothing can harm him because he has this protection, a thing that he puts on himself and wears around his neck. He could come into the church and say that he has not converted and then he has a handkerchief or I don't know whatever [the Vodou priest or priestess] gave him. He believes in the object, it's his protection [against harm]. At the same time the young man comes inside a church, he listens to [the sermon for the day], and he believes that the thing around his neck from Haiti will protect him. Whereas a person who is Christian, he/she is not like that. The only protection he/she has is in God, understand?[22]

Brother Nicholas contends that a *Kretyen* is different from a *Pwotestan* because the Christian does not believe in the spiritual power that a Vodou priest or priestess can access or place in amulets. Brother Nicholas also discursively constructs himself as a Christian by stating that he would not go to *kay gangan* (a Vodou priest's place of work). By discussing someone who actually went to Haiti, bought an amulet, and came back to the Bahamas confident that nothing could harm him, Brother Nicholas presented himself as a *Kretyen* because a Christian understands that the only protection he or she has is God, the sole source of their faith.[23]

The Importance of *Kretyen* and Haitian Protestant Nationalism

The work of anthropologist Nina Glick Schiller and education professor Georges Fouron on long-distance nationalism sheds light on why some Haitian Protestants living outside the borders of Haiti create the moral boundaries of *Kretyen* and *Pwotestan*. Drawing from Victor Turner's approach to symbols as resources deployed by social actors, Glick Schiller and Fouron (2001, 28) note that ideologies, such as nationalism, can be understood as "discursive formations" in which shared sets of symbols contain multiple meanings and messages. They also observe that "the nation is in many ways a 'floating signifier'—that is, it means contradictory things to people who organize to obtain diametrically different views of the future, all waving the national flag." The word *polysemous*, which one can understand as "having a multiplicity of meanings," is also important to understand the power of nationalist ideologies. *Polysemous* highlights the flexibility of nationalism in that it can readily encompass religious messages about personal or collective salvation in discussions about the future of the nation.

Based on Glick Schiller and Fouron's contributions to our understanding of nationalism—and keeping in mind that devout Haitian Protestant Christians are operating within a transnational social field that includes Haiti, the Bahamas, and the United States—the answer to the importance of the identity of *Kretyen* lies outside of the borders of the Bahamas and leads us to Haiti. When the appearance and behavior of Haitian Protestant migrants are perceived to have gone awry, it is evidence that the salvation of the offenders is in question. For many, the appearance and behavior of Haiti as a nation has gone awry. In Haiti, the average observer sees environmental degradation, governmental instability, crime, and widespread poverty as common occurrences. The 2010 earthquake magnified these issues even more. Additionally, as Glick Schiller and Fouron (2001, 61) note, each Haitian not only represents his or her own family, but also the nation of Haiti wherever he or she goes. In this sense, one can understand why devout Haitian Protestant Christians in New Providence believe that the salvation and future of Haiti are in question.[24]

The link between a person's individual salvation and the salvation of Haiti as a nation is revealed through the ways in which devout Haitian Protestant migrants discuss approaches to the resolution of the socioeconomic crisis facing Haiti. I asked research consultants two questions concerning Haiti and contemporary Haitian society: What is your view of the current social situation in Haiti (Sò panse de sitiasyon sosyal nan Ayiti)? What does Haiti need to change its current social situation (Sò panse Ayiti bezwen pou chanje sitiasyon sosyal li)? In response to the first question, the majority of respondents described the country's situation in negative terms, conveying despair that Haiti's economic, social, and political problems may never be resolved. When answering the second question, the majority of research consultants responded "selman Bondyè kapab chanje Ayiti [only God can change Haiti]." By invoking and linking God to the amelioration of life in Haiti, following, submitting to, and fearing a Protestant Christian God becomes the only way for Haiti's endemic poverty to be eradicated and for the nation to stabilize economically and politically so that some can eventually return to their homeland.

In the opinion of devout Haitian Protestant Christians, Haiti's salvation lies in Christ, and the transformation of Haiti into a stable nation-state lies in the acceptance of ideals and morals that are associated with what it means to be a *Kretyen*. When the members of Haitian Baptist, Interdenominational, Nazarene and Pentecostal churches of New Providence sing hymns of national pride and pray for *yon chanjman* (a positive change) to Haiti's current crisis, the identities *Kretyen* and *Pwotestan* must be seen as "part of a much larger set of actions expressing love for God and church and, by extension, for nation" (Butler 2002, 116). When Protestants profess to be Christian but appear or behave in ways that are antithetical to the type of Christianity they supposedly practice, they delay their personal salvation as well as the salvation of Haiti from endemic poverty, crime, governmental inefficiency, and overall misery. Thus, the offensive behavior and appearance of a Protestant is more than a faux pas. It manifests the symbolic boundary of the *Pwotestan* rather than the ideal religious identity that devout Haitian Protestants try to achieve and that they see as the ideal citizen of Haiti: *Kretyen*.

Improper comportment and appearance among Haitian Protestant migrants reflects the type of citizen that *Kretyen* Haitian migrants consider to be at the foundation of the current crisis in Haiti. *Kretyen* Haitian migrants believe that when Haitian citizens practice retribution instead of loving their neighbors, they make life in Haiti difficult. The Haitian head-of-state who embezzles foreign aid funds for personal use, as in the case of the Duvalier regime, is what *Kretyen* Haitians in New Providence believe is wrong with Haiti. Haitian citizens who practice Vodou and poison or use *maji* to eliminate their enemies contribute to the perpetuation of the crisis in Haiti. A *Kretyen* president, they believe, would dedicate the country of Haiti to Jesus Christ, and not consider Vodou as a religion on equal footing with Catholicism and Protestantism, as former President Jean-Bertrand Aristide did in 2003 when he recognized Vodou as an official religion of Haiti. Haitian government employees who accept bribes in return for political favors are likewise not the types of citizens that help Haiti become a nation to which its diaspora can return. Those types of citizens are morally corrupt, like *Pwotestan* Haitian migrants.

In the diasporic religious community of Haitian Protestant migrants, then, maintaining the external and observable aspects of a religious culture developed in Haiti, which includes an austere dress code and abstaining from sinful behavior such as premarital sex and *plasaj*, demonstrates the behavior of a *krent pou Bondyè*—that one is *Kretyen*, and that one embodies the qualities of the ideal citizen for Haiti. God is the supreme force in devout Haitian Protestant migrants' lives that they fear and respect. These migrants believe God should be at the head of the Haitian state, as expressed in the refrain of French hymn 320 in Chants d'espérance mentioned earlier: "Save, Lord, / bless our dear Haiti! / Small nation, advance toward Zion. / Devote yourself to God. / Make Jesus your King, / Save, O Lord, / bless our beloved Haiti!" Being a *Kretyen* is not only the more attractive religious identity in their view, but also the sole identity that holds the key to transforming Haiti for the better. An example from ethnomusicologist Melvin Butler's work among Haitian Pentecostals illustrates this point about the link between an individual's salvation and the national salvation of Haiti.

In his ethnomusicology study of Haitian Pentecostal worship within a transnational social field, Butler (2002, 116) studied Haitian Pentecostal churches in New York City and Jacmel, Haiti. He found that among *Kor de Kri* (Body of Christ) Pentecostals in Haiti, their use of American styles of music in services—rather than the use of the popular Haitian style of music called *konpa*[25]—demonstrated a simultaneous distancing from the secular Haitian world and a step toward personal salvation and national salvation for Haiti. For Pentecostals to live victoriously on earth they must be empowered by the Holy Spirit to resist sin and worldly temptations, derive joy from a personal relationship with God, and grow stronger through life's adversities. Because popular Haitian dance bands that sing about carnal pleasures and other vices of the secular world play *konpa*, worship in this musical style represents a potential spiritual hindrance to Body of Christ Pentecostals. When Body of Christ Pentecostals use American styles of music in their services, then, it is in the belief that they are ensuring their individual salvation and national salvation for Haiti (116).

Similarly Haitian Protestant Christian transmigrants use the ways that Protestant Christianity is practiced in Haiti both as a model for normative religious behavior in the Bahamas and as a symbol for what is lacking in Haiti. Pious *Kretyen* behavior and austere *Kretyen* appearance reflect the basis of a political critique that my research consultants in New Providence's Haitian Protestant community believe to be necessary for personal salvation. The identity of *Kretyen* reflects the ultimate hope for devout Haitian Protestant migrants for the future of Haiti. Their commitment to defending the Haitian Protestant tradition in the Bahamas thus can also be viewed as a form of nationalism.

There are three forms of nationalism among devout Haitian Protestant migrants.[26] First, there is the border-crossing nationalism of Haitian transmigrants in response to their experiences in the Bahamas. The most undesirable nationality for any person living in the Bahamas is Haitian, but Haitians view Haitianness with varying degrees of pride whereas Bahamians of Haitian descent mostly view their Haitian parentage as a hindrance that prevents them from full inclusion in Bahamian society. Bahamians of Haitian descent try to reconcile this contradiction but the Haitian nationality that the Bahamian state ascribes to them prevents them from being fully integrated and accepted as fellow Bahamians in Bahamian society.

The second form of nationalism comes from the complex relationship Haitians in the Bahamas maintain to Haiti—one in which familial obligations, memory, pride, and despair are all intertwined. The experiences of exploitation, marginalization, and segregation in the Bahamas shape Haitian memories of and longing for Haiti.

The third form of nationalism that Haitian Protestant migrants practice is Protestant Christianity as nationalism, specifically, the maintenance of religious customs and beliefs relating to comportment and dress that reflect what it means to be a devout Protestant Christian: the best type of Haitian citizen. Living life as a *Kretyen*—not as a *Pwotestan*—is not only the key to survival for Haitian Protestant migrants but also the key to transforming Haiti, through the power of God and its citizens, from the poorest country in the Western Hemisphere to a nation where Haitians can lead dignified lives. Personal salvation and transformation attest to the power of God in one's life and how that divine force can transform a nation that is *tet anba* (upside down). This is important to recognize considering that most Haitian Protestant migrants in the Bahamas who were interviewed for this study could not or did not want to go back to Haiti and their only contact with Haiti was through traditional forms of communication. The nationalism they developed in New Providence, through their use of *Kretyen* and *Pwotestan* symbolic boundaries, reflects their aspirations and hopes for a new type of citizen in Haiti. Their hope is that more citizens of Haiti will convert to Protestant forms of Christianity, leave Vodou behind, and become *Kretyen* by developing a comportment shaped by Haitian Protestant culture, fixing their appearance as a way of demonstrating a true spiritual transformation, and developing a conscience that demonstrates their *krent pou Bondyè*.

Protestantism in the Haitian diaspora of the Bahamas practiced in this manner, then, is a form of nationalism in that prayer and adherence to the cultural norms and behavior of Protestant culture as practiced in Haiti seeks to influence a transformation in Haitian citizenry. It is a nationalism that aims to construct a new state in Haiti based on religious beliefs and practices that symbolize religious purity and a cultural identity that will ultimately transform Haiti into an economically viable and politically stable nation-state.

Conclusion

Modernity Revisited

If my people, which are called by my name, shall humble
themselves, and pray and seek my face, and turn from their
wicked ways. Then I will hear from heaven, and will forgive
their sin, and will heal their land.

The Holy Bible, 2 Chronicles 7.14

In the fields of anthropology and religious studies, many generally
assume that being a Protestant or being a Christian is one and the same
identity. However, by applying symbolic boundary theory, we recognize
that Protestant Christian identity is a complex construct. This ethnography's use of symbolic boundary theory, which integrates an intellectualist
approach and transnationalism theory, articulates why Haitians remain
devout Protestant Christians rather than switching among Protestantism,
Catholicism, and Vodou. This approach also explains why migrants draw
the symbolic boundaries of *Kretyen*, *Pwotestan*, and *moun ki poko konvèti*, and why they reject Vodou. While this book uses symbolic boundary theory to understand Haitian religious practices, symbolic boundary
theory can also be used to study contemporary religious change in different cultural contexts within the Caribbean and Latin America and other
regions. Furthermore, using symbolic boundary theory contributes to
the larger discussion in anthropology and religious studies about Christian identity, diaspora Christianity, transnational religious migration,
and contemporary religious change. Through symbolic boundary work,

devout Haitian Protestants in the Bahamas also demonstrate how transnationalism, nationalism, and migration are intertwined in the views of their diasporic religious community.

This ethnography also builds on recent advancements in the anthropology and sociology of Christianity—including intellectualist approaches that emphasize how people make meaning out of Protestant Christianity (Austin-Broos 1997; Brusco 1995; Cannell 2006; Guadeloupe 2009; Harding 1987; 1991; 2000; Keane 2007; Robbins 2004a/b)—and an understanding that Protestant Christianity is not just an extension of American religious imperialism or European colonialism. Utilitarian approaches to the study of Christianity highlight practical factors that influence conversion to Christianity and are drawn on mainly to answer why people in underdeveloped countries convert. The intellectualist approach emphasizes a gradual break with a premodern past and a reorientation of a person's worldview to the religion he or she converted to. This book's contribution to the growing body of work in the anthropology of Christianity is a nuanced approach that uses an intellectualist framework to understand the use of *Kretyen* and *Pwotestan* by devout Haitian Protestant migrants. In particular, many of the research consultants interviewed used an intellectualist approach to determine who within their diasporic religious community goes to church to do everything but embody the word of a Protestant God in their everyday lives. These ideas are realized and described through symbolic boundaries that reflect their worldview as it is structured according to their religious beliefs. By discursively constructing offenders of unwritten cultural rules as *Pwotestan* while simultaneously casting themselves as *Kretyen*, devout Haitian Protestant migrants emphasize and reflect intellectualist analysis.

This study also contributes to the transnational migration literature (see Basch et al. 1994; Tsuda 2003; and Rouse 1991) because it focuses on transnational relationships in a receiving country other than the United States. Earlier ethnographies about the Haitian diaspora have focused on Haitian communities in the United States and how they are connected to Haiti through remittances (see Glick Schiller and Fouron 2001; Stepick

1998). Over time the geographical focus on the United States has come to define the Haitian transnational experience when in fact there are Haitian diasporas throughout North America and the Caribbean that are structured differently due to the societal contexts of receiving countries like the Bahamas (St. Jacques 2001). This ethnography also contributes to transnational religious migration theory (Ebaugh and Chafetz 2002; Mooney 2009; Richman 2005a) by arguing for the use of symbolic boundary theory and intellectualist approaches in the study of transnational religious migration to provide an emic perspective of an under-researched religious movement gaining traction within a transnational social space.

Furthermore, this book attempts to swing the pendulum of Haitian religious studies away from Vodou and Catholicism and toward the growing practice of Protestant forms of Christianity. As I have argued, traditional studies of the religions Haitians practice have tended to pay more attention to Vodou and Catholicism and less attention to Protestant Christianity. The continued research focus on Catholicism and Vodou in anthropology and religious studies tends to misrepresent contemporary Haitian religious practice as more Haitians, as this ethnography has shown, are practicing Protestant forms of Christianity. Furthermore, when there is scholarly attention devoted to the study of Haitian Protestantism, it tends to emphasize utilitarian explanations for the existence and spread of Protestantism among Haitians. Although utilitarian motives, such as relief from illness, convince many Haitians to convert to Protestant forms of Christianity, many Haitians develop a worldview that is intellectualist in its foundation. Thus, a sustained ethnographic attention to this transnational religious movement is necessary to understand Protestantism's persuasion to Haitians and why Protestant Christianity may be the majority religion in other diasporic milieus such as Miami, Florida, and Boston, Massachusetts.

Finally, this ethnography is a contribution to recent studies that acknowledge that Haitian Protestantism is growing and deserves ethnographic attention due to the way in which it is altering the religious landscape of Haiti and Haitian diasporic milieus (Brodwin 2003b; Butler 2002; Conway 1978; Germain 2011; Louis, Jr. 2010; 2011; 2012; McAlister 2012; and Richman 2002a/b; 2012). This ethnography introduces Haitian Protestantism to the fields of anthropology and religious studies, calls for more sustained ethnographic attention to this religion of choice for Haitians at home and abroad, and raises awareness about the political implications of the practice of Protestant forms of Christianity in the Caribbean and Latin America. Haitian Protestantism is no longer invisible.

Toward a Better Future

In the introduction I mention anthropologist Webb Keane's views regarding modernity. Keane (2007, 48) argues that the idea of modernity includes two distinctive features: rupture from a traditional past and progress into a better future. For some devout Haitian Protestant migrants, rupture from a traditional past means breaking away from Catholic and Vodou traditions. At its foundation, progress into a better future for all Haitians begins, in their view, with proper appearance and comportment that mirrors the culture of Protestant Christianity as it is practiced in Haiti.

Diasporic Haitian Protestantism, then, can be viewed as a political critique of Haitian society and the Haitian citizen. To reiterate, traditional religion (Vodou) and the majority religion of Haiti (Catholicism) have not solved Haiti's past and present problems as the poorest country in the Western Hemisphere. The traditional ways of doing things in Haiti have failed and there is only one path toward a better future for Haitians in Haiti: they have to become devout Protestant Christians. In other words, Haitians must reject their African roots, put the God of Protestant Christianity at the head of the nation, and submit the country to the God of Protestant Christianity. Haitian Protestantism, then, can be seen as a project that has as its goal to integrate Haiti as a respected nation among nations through a global Christian identity. To be *Kretyen* means to be a new citizen who possesses the habits and qualities that allow Haiti to be a functional country. Protestantism in the Haitian diaspora of the Bahamas practiced in this manner, then, becomes a form of nationalist expression. Specifically, migrant Protestantism seeks to transform Haiti in a positive way through the practice of "authentic" forms of Haitian Protestantism, which are based on religious beliefs and practices that symbolize religious purity and a new citizen. These beliefs and practices are meant to transform Haiti into an economically viable and politically stable nation-state, like the Bahamas.

Christianity is a core element of Bahamian national identity. As historians Michael Craton and Gail Saunders (1998, 444) write, "to a people who are at least as religious as they are political, the churches have been almost as important as the government in defining and defending national identity and traditional cultural values." The Bahamas is over 96 percent Christian and Bahamians attend Baptist, Roman Catholic, Anglican, Methodist, Church of God, and Pentecostal churches on a regular basis.[1] Aspects of Christianity are weaved into Bahamian culture and are a common part of many daily activities. For example, you will find a religion section and Bible verses in daily Bahamian newspapers. Also, government programs and events usually open with a prayer. In short, Christianity is central to what it means to be a Bahamian. Many Bahamians believe that part of their prosperity comes from the fact that their country is a Christian nation that places God first. Devout Haitian Protestants share the belief that when God comes first in Haiti, Haiti will become a prosperous and stable nation-state. This is important lest they, and Haiti, incur the wrath of an angry God, as the following anecdote from the field demonstrates.

On Sunday, September 11, 2005, I visited a Bahamian church that offered a Creole service for Haitians. Brother Immaculé, who was from Haiti and sometimes attended International Tabernacle of Praise, had invited me to come to his church the week before, when I was conducting an interview with Sister Maude. Although an 8 am service was early for me (I planned on attending a service at Victory Chapel later that day), I decided to attend because I had heard of Bahamian churches with Haitian services and wanted to witness a service like this firsthand.

I remember that day as a melancholy one. It was the fourth anniversary of the 9/11 attacks in the United States which destroyed the Twin Towers in New York City, damaged the Pentagon outside of Washington, DC, and killed more Americans on a flight that ended tragically in Pennsylvania. Just a few weeks earlier, Hurricane Katrina had made landfall in the Gulf Coast region, leaving many Americans dead, displaced, or stuck in their cities and towns. I felt sad because the anniversary of the 9/11 attacks and the unfolding tragedies in the wake of Hurricane Katrina were exacerbated by living in Bahamian society that was hostile to foreigners, including myself, a black American of Haitian descent.

Brother Immaculé picked me up early from my apartment and dropped me off at the Church of God of Prophecy on Baillou Hill Road. According to the institution's website, the Church of God of Prophecy movement, which began in the rural mountains of Cherokee County, North Carolina, is a "Protestant, Evangelical, Wesleyan holiness, Pentecostal movement that believes in man's freewill regarding salvation." The spiritual pioneers of the church trace their roots to "the New Testament church and consider themselves a continuation of the Spirit-filled Christianity exhibited in the book of Acts."[2]

As I stepped into the sanctuary I looked around and counted how many people were present (about fifteen to twenty, mostly Bahamian) and then took a seat. I immediately kneeled and prayed for families affected by the September 11 anniversary, Hurricane Katrina, myself, and my family. I then read some of the Bible verses posted around the pulpit. A pastor from the church read Psalm 1 in English. While he reminded us to be appreciative of our blessings, he said something about Hurricane Katrina in New Orleans that took me by surprise at the time. The pastor said that because New Orleans has gambling, prostitution, and other Bacchanalian activities, the city's wickedness had brought the catastrophe upon itself. This comment was echoed by Brother Immaculé later on during the service when he preached in English from 2 Chronicles

7.14—"If my people, which are called by my name, shall humble themselves, and pray and seek my face, and turn from their wicked ways. Then I will hear from heaven, and will forgive their sin, and will heal their land."—and reinforced the view that the victims of Hurricane Katrina in the Gulf Coast region, most notably the ungodliness of the people of New Orleans, Louisiana, had caused God's wrath. Brother Immaculé supported his analysis with Malachi 3.6—"I am the Lord and do not change"—to remind the congregation that the God of the Old Testament is still the same God of today and one should be careful to avoid committing wicked acts as the people of the Gulf Coast supposedly did. The English-speaking members of the congregation received his sermon enthusiastically. After Brother Immaculé's sermon, I was invited to the pulpit to address the congregation and I asked them to pray for the victims of the September 11 attacks and Hurricane Katrina before I returned to my seat.

Brother Immaculé's 2005 interpretation of Hurricane Katrina as God's judgment raining down on the "wicked" people of the Gulf Coast region of the United States resonates with Pat Robertson's comments about Haiti's pact with the Devil in the wake of the 2010 earthquake in Haiti, and similar sentiments voiced by devout Haitian Protestant migrants. The symbolic boundaries of *Kretyen* and *Pwotestan* also resonate with the Bahamian Christian distinction that there is a difference between a Christian and people who are "playing church"—that is, going through the motions of what it may outwardly mean to be a Christian but are still committing egregious sins by Bahamian Christian standards. Since they are Christians, Haitian Protestant migrants could be integrated into a larger, Christian Bahamas. But at the time of my research, the general Bahamian populace was unaware that the majority of Haitians in the Bahamas are Protestant Christians and that there were more than twenty Haitian Protestant churches in New Providence. How can this be, given the similar worldviews, experiences, and centrality of religion to Haitian Protestant migrants and Bahamian Christians? Why do Haitian Protestant migrants continue to remain on the margins of Bahamian Christian society? Put differently, since Bahamians practice Christianity, and the majority of Haitian migrants in the Bahamas practice Protestant Christianity, why do Bahamians refuse to accept Haitians as fellow Christians?

My research suggests that despite sharing a similar Christian worldview, Haitian Protestants will not be accepted as fellow Christians by the majority of Bahamians because of their desire to keep the Bahamas for Bahamians at all costs. This reality trumps any potential collective religious solidarity between Christian Bahamians and Protestant Haitians that could ensure that the majority of Haitians in the Bahamas would be treated as the equals of Bahamians. Therefore, Haitians must be refracted through a prism of policy and propaganda that distorts the way they are perceived. Through Bahamian power, Haitians are transformed into inferior beings that are viewed throughout the Bahamas as repugnant others which, in turn, justifies their overall exploitation. The Christian identity of Haitian Protestants in the Bahamas, which should allow them to be accepted and not marginalized among Bahamian Christians, is overshadowed, nullified, and erased by Bahamian social and political constructions of Haitians as disruptive parasites who supposedly bring the perceived social chaos of Haiti with them when they migrate to the Bahamas.

As a result of the laws and structure of Bahamian society, the stereotypes about Haitian migrants and their progeny will continue to endure, Haitians will continue to accept the indignities associated with daily life in the Bahamas, the progeny of Haitians in the Bahamas will continue to despise their Haitian nationality, and the core elements of Bahamian identity will continue to be blackness (with a proper, Bahamian surname), Christianity, and xenophobia. In this context, Haitians will never have the same rights as Bahamians do in Bahamian society. Then why do Haitian Protestants maintain their practice of Protestant Christianity, which resonates with aspects of Bahamian Christianity, even though they can never become full citizens of Bahamian society?

Devout Haitian Protestant migrants maintain their practice of Protestant Christianity because it serves as a coping mechanism as they deal with the exploitation and marginalization they experience in the Bahamas. They would rather pay bribes to the police to stay out of jail and go without any pay after a week's work than be threatened with deportation to Haiti. Thus, their practice of Protestant Christianity is a way to tolerate the daily indignities they experience. And some Haitian Protestants in the Bahamas practice their form of Christianity also because of the spiritual effects they believe they could have on transforming Haiti into a respected, dignified nation where people have hope for a viable future.

Whether they go to the United States or stay in the Bahamas, many Haitian migrants would like Haiti to become a nation where people can live their lives with dignity. Migrant life in the Bahamas prevents them from doing so because of humiliating exploitation and marginalization. After the friend of a church brother at New Haitian Mission Baptist Church was arrested and deported, another church brother told me that he would prefer to be back in Haiti where the specter of arrest and deportation did not exist. Those who prefer to migrate to the United States would still like to see life in Haiti improve so that their relatives can lead dignified lives. I asked all my Haitian migrant research consultants if they would like to continue to live in the Bahamas, return to Haiti, or move elsewhere. Brother Jean-Baptiste, who attended International Tabernacle of Praise at that time, answered, "kò m Nasò, men lespri mwen Ayiti," which meant that although his body was in Nassau (New Providence), his spirit was in Haiti.[3] Haiti is where his wife and two sons live and it is there where he feels most comfortable. Comments such as these not only express nostalgia for a homeland but also anticipate a day when he and other migrants can return to a country where they will find gainful employment and support themselves and their kin so that they can remain there permanently. But the Haiti crisis forces Brother Jean-Baptiste and other Haitians to live in a foreign country to earn a living to support their loved ones.

For devout Haitian Protestant migrants, who would like to return permanently to Haiti, many believe that they can only go back to a country that has been transformed through the catalytic action of the Holy Spirit.

Those migrants who reject Vodou, and anything else that symbolically reflects Africa, offer a different reading of Haitian society than Haitian Catholics and Vodou practitioners while at the same time trying to realize the goal of the Haitian Revolution: to dismantle the previous oppressive society and replace it with a new one where all Haitians have the opportunity to lead a dignified life. This Haitian Protestant approach, however, is radically different from approaches that have come before it, and it resonates with the rejection of traditional, creolized, and indigenous religions that is apparent with the Protestant transformation of the Caribbean and Latin America (see Austin-Broos 1997; Brusco 1995). Devout Haitian Protestantism is growing in popularity as the religious movement grows within postearthquake Haiti and in diasporic contexts.

As long as ecological, economic, and societal degradation occurs in Haiti, Haitians will continue to migrate to the Bahamas and elsewhere in search of a better life and to meet kin obligations. And as long as Haiti remains in a crisis, some devout Haitian Protestants will strive to be *Kretyen* to serve as an example of what Haiti's ideal citizen should be like. By wearing the proper attire and behaving in a way recognized as pious by Protestant Christians in Haiti through their *krent pou Bondyè*, devout Haitian Protestant migrants have faith that one day Haiti will become a Protestant Christian nation where peace and prosperity reign and will be accepted as an equal member among nations around the world.

NOTES

INTRODUCTION

1. Since many Haitians live in the Bahamas as undocumented migrants, I have changed the names of the Haitian Protestant participants I interviewed to protect their identities. I have also changed the names of the progeny of Haitian migrants in the Bahamas and the name of the Bahamian informant. Brother Magloire, interview with the author, New Providence, Bahamas, November 8, 2005.

2. Haitians from Protestant Christian traditions sometimes use the term *evangelical* to refer to themselves, like in the United States.

3. I thank Dr. Randall Hepner for suggesting the term *twin barbarisms*.

4. Seasoning was a violent disciplining process intended to modify the behavior and attitude of slaves and transform them into effective laborers. The power relations between the Africans who became slaves and the interests of plantation commodity production together formed a process that transformed diverse Africans into slaves. In some cases, seasoning lasted up to two years.

5. The figure is most likely higher. In the Bureau of Applied Research in Anthropology (BARA) Baseline Study of Livelihood Security in the Departments of the Artibonite, Center, North, Northeast, and West (1997), Woodson et al. observed that Haitian conversion to Protestant forms of Christianity was one of the most significant religious changes in the Adventist Development and Relief Agency's zone of intervention in the last thirty years (98). In four departments, 20 to 25 percent of the household heads were Protestant, but the figure rose to 38.7 percent in the west (98).

A 1996 BARA study on the Southern Peninsula of Haiti yielded similar results (55–56). In fact, there were some areas in Southern Haiti where the percentage of Protestant households were 42.9 percent (Bois La Rue), 55.6 percent (Aréguy), 51.4 percent (Potier), and 100 percent (Boleau).

Finally, a study on culture in Port-au-Prince observed that in 1996 approximately 39 percent of Port-au-Prince was Protestant (François and Rémy 1997, 38–39).

6. Stepick and Portes (1986, 345) also found that during the 1980s, a third of Haitian refugees in Miami, Florida, were Protestant.

7. The Haitian population of the Bahamas is estimated to be between 30,000 to 60,000 people. The overall population of the Bahamas is approximately 324,834

according to the CIA World Factbook, https://www.cia.gov/library/publications/
the-world-factbook/geos/bf.html.

8. According to the website of the 700 Club, "*The 700 Club* can be seen in 96 percent of the homes in the U.S. and is carried on ABC Family cable network, FamilyNet,
Trinity Broadcasting Network, plus numerous local U.S. television stations, and is seen
daily by approximately one million viewers. CBN [Christian Broadcasting Network]
International maintains 15 television production centers around the world that create
indigenous versions of The 700 Club and other Christian programs in 39 languages.
CBN International programs are broadcast in 138 countries to an estimated yearly
viewing audience of 360 million people," http://www.cbn.com/700club/ShowInfo/
About/about700club.aspx.

9. See "Robertson's "true story": Haiti "swore a pact to the devil" to get "free from
the French" and "ever since, they have been cursed," *Media Matters*, January 13, 2010,
http://mediamatters.org/mmtv/201001130024.

10. I theorize that an unintended consequence of the limitations Bahamian society
puts on Haitians who migrate to the Bahamas is the growth of Evangelical Protestantism among Haitians in the Bahamas. The creation of new churches and congregations
is fueled by the exclusion of Haitians in the political processes in the Bahamas and the
lack of prestigious employment opportunities available to Haitians (specifically Haitian
men) in the Bahamas.

11. Actions de Grâces à L'Éternel is a participatory event where the people who are
present sing songs from Protestant hymnody in French and Haitian Creole, read Old
and New Testament passages from the Holy Bible, pray for one another, preach and
provide testimonials about the positive effects God can have on a person's life as long
as they follow the word of God as written in the Holy Bible. Within my family, Actions
de Grâces began in Haiti and coincided with a service performed by American missionaries in the 1950s during the time when Thanksgiving is observed in the United
States. Soeur (Sister) Jonas, as Alice Fougy was known as in Haitian Protestant circles,
adopted the idea of Thanksgiving as a way for her kin and fictive kin—brothers and
sisters in Christ—to meet in worship. My family would travel from Staten Island, New
York, to Washington, DC, for example, in September and November for Actions de
Grâces.

12. I also participated in a variety of other Protestant church activities. For example,
I went to another Actions de Grâces at L'Église de Saint-Paul (Saint Paul's Church),
an African Methodist Episcopal Church in Port-au-Prince. This service took a similar
form as the service in Ti Rivye, Jacmel. I attended four morning services of the First
Baptist Church of Port-au-Prince, Reunion Street. Those services resonated with
Actions de Grâces services I had attended earlier. The major differences were: (1) the
dominant use of French in preaching and hymn singing, although Haitian Creole
hymns were sung at times (this represented a class dimension that became apparent to
me once I attended subsequent services), and (2) gender roles: only men preached and

collected donations from congregants. The final activity at the First Baptist Church of Port-au-Prince at Reunion Street I attended was a Baptist funeral for one of its female congregants who lived to be eighty-eight years old. The funeral was well attended and the role of women at the service centered on the women's choir and a more active role in reading Bible passages and singing solos from the pulpit. The service was held predominantly in French as were other services at this church.

I also visited Radio Lumière ("The Light" Radio), a Protestant radio station that reaches 95 percent of Haiti, 25 percent of the Dominican Republic, and 5 percent of Cuba. I learned about the history of the radio station from its director. I also interviewed a video technician about one of the station's new enterprises: Télévision Lumière. They have a huge impact in spreading Protestant gospel all over Haiti. I also took Haitian Creole lessons to improve my writing, reading, and speaking skills.

13. I use the terms *informants, interviewees,* and *research consultants* interchangeably.

14. Dieunous Senatus, interview with the author, New Providence, Bahamas, August 8, 2005.

15. I make my own distinction between Haitians, people born in Haiti and then migrate to the Bahamas, and Bahamians of Haitian descent, children of Haitian descent who are born in the Bahamas, to help readers differentiate between the two culturally distinct groups. Although both groups are recognized socially as Haitians, those who are from Haiti speak Haitian Creole and French whereas their children, who have grown up in the Bahamas, usually have English as their first language and acquire Haitian Creole later in life, sometimes through socialization at Catholic and Protestant churches.

Also, in my earlier work (see Louis 2012), I referred to Bahamians of Haitian descent as Haitian-Bahamians. This term is inaccurate because a person is either Bahamian or Haitian in Bahamian society.

16. I asked the first two Bahamians of Haitian descent I interviewed these questions. They answered that they were Christian and never heard about the distinction that Haitian Protestants make between *Pwotestan* and *Kretyen.*

CHAPTER 1. HAITIAN PROTESTANT CULTURE

1. Some discussions in this chapter are updated and reworked from material that originally appeared in Louis (2012b). *"Touloutoutou* and *Tet Mare* Churches: Language, Class and Protestantism in the Haitian Diaspora of the Bahamas," *Studies in Religion/ Sciences Religieuses* 41, no. 2 (June 2012), 216–230; published online before print on April 18, 2012, doi: 10.1177/0008429812441308.

2. I distinguish between Haitians who are born and raised in Haiti and Haitians who are born in the Bahamas.

3. Sister Maude, interview with the author, New Providence, Bahamas. September 6, 2005.

4. Ibid.

5. Many Haitians and Bahamians refer to the island of New Providence as Nassau, the capital of the Bahamas.

6. Sister Ann, interview with the author, New Providence, Bahamas, July 13, 2005.

7. An example of this belief can be found in John 3:18–19 (Holy Bible, New Living Translation): "Dear children, let us stop just saying we love each other; let us really show it by our actions. It is by our actions that we know we are living in truth, so we will be confident when we stand before the Lord."

8. See Genesis 32:22–32: "But during the night Jacob got up and sent his two wives, two concubines, and eleven sons across the Jabbok River. After they were on the other side, he sent over all his possessions. This left Jacob all alone in the camp, and a man came and wrestled with him until dawn. When the man saw that he couldn't win the match, he struck Jacob's hip and knocked it out of joint at the socket. Then the man said, 'Let me go, for it is dawn.' But Jacob panted, 'I will not let you go unless you bless me.' 'What is your name?' the man asked. He replied 'Jacob.' 'Your name will no longer be Jacob,' the man told him. 'It is now Israel, because you have struggled both with God and men and have won.' 'What is your name?' Jacob asked him. 'Why do you ask?' the man replied. Then he blessed Jacob there. Jacob named the place Peniel—'face of God'—for he said, 'I have seen God's face to face, yet my life has been spared.' The sun rose as he left Peniel, and he was limping because of his hip. That is why even today the people of Israel don't eat meat from near the hip, in memory of what happened that night."

9. Field notes from International Tabernacle of Praise Ministries full immersion baptism at Montagu Bay, New Providence, Bahamas, October 16, 2005.

10. One informant from New Mission, who was a member at a *Kor de Kri* (Body of Christ) Pentecostal church in Northern Haiti, explained to me how he converted at a morning church service and was baptized the same day in an afternoon baptismal service at a river.

11. Part of the tradition of Haitian Protestantism is to have only members of the church partake in *lasentsen* rather than members and nonmembers as is the case in the United States, for example. Not all of them are baptized. In Haiti some churches have the believers go outside to wait for their families and friends who are inside participating in the ceremonial drinking the blood of Christ and eating His flesh.

12. This was in stark contrast to the Adventist Church, the Church of Jesus Christ of Latter-day Saints, and the Kingdom Hall of Jehovah's Witnesses that had Haitian members and did not take part in any interdenominational activities with the greater Haitian Protestant community.

13. A difference between Victory Chapel and the other two churches was based on the Nazarene emphasis on sanctification and holiness. Whereas the doctrine of New Mission was based on Union of Evangelical Baptists in Haiti (UEBH) principles and International Tabernacle of Praise had yet to decide on the four principles that characterize Protestantism in Haiti, the doctrine of Victory Chapel Church of the Nazarene was distinct. The Church of Nazarene denomination emphasizes the Methodist and

Wesleyan concepts of sanctification and holiness. Stressing sanctification and holiness means that although they accepted Christ as their personal savior, they are an unfinished product. In other words, the Nazarenes believe that they must meditate and continually strive toward these two principles while on earth.

14. With regard to language use in Haiti, the country can best be described as a nation predominantly composed of two linguistic communities: a minority French bilingual elite and a monolingual Creole-speaking majority. In their study of orthographic debates over the written representation of the spoken language of Haitian Creole, linguistic anthropologists Bambi Schieffelin and Rachelle Doucet (1994, 178) remark that Haitian French was viewed as the high prestige form of language while Creole was considered the low prestige form. For example, the use of French as a language of communication and transactions in Haiti is not only viewed as a symbol of education and refinement but also is a form of symbolic capital that is transferable to employment opportunities within different settings in Haitian society. For instance, higher education in Haiti is conducted in French and students take their exams, write papers, and question and respond to their instructors in French. Transactions between tellers and customers at banks are conducted largely in French. Subsequently, if a person wants to become a teacher, a doctor, or a lawyer, or have investments in a local bank in Haiti, that person must be fluent in French. French in Haiti, then, is the language of upward mobility that Haitians of all classes use to ascend a highly stratified society and solidify their class position.

15. *Solanelman* in Haitian Creole means solemnly, ceremoniously, seriously, with reverence.

16. Sister Edwidge, interview with the author, New Providence, Bahamas, August 12, 2005.

17. As there are two major forms of Protestantism in Haiti, there are at least two types of Baptist churches in Haiti: traditional (Puritanical) and charismatic. The traditional type of Baptist church in Haiti is very reserved and can be characterized as a *touloutoutou* church. The charismatic variants of Baptist churches in Haiti are characterized as *tet mare* churches.

18. Sister Edwidge, interview.

19. Traditionally, men are the only individuals who can become pastors in traditional Baptist churches in Haiti revealing a gender hierarchy that reflects indigenous patriarchy. Women are allowed to preach on special occasions at the First Baptist Church of Port-au-Prince but they are not allowed to become pastors. The highest position a woman can obtain within this hierarchy is *dam misyonè* (missionary lady) or evangelist.

20. The Union of Evangelical Baptists in Haiti (UEBH) is a fellowship of Baptist churches established in 1928. The churches convene and agree on the doctrine that all churches within the union should follow.

21. Brother Bicha, interview with the author, New Providence, Bahamas, November 9, 2005.

CHAPTER 2. HAITIANS IN THE BAHAMAS

1. This chapter is an updated version of my previously published article, "The Haitian Diaspora of the Bahamas: An Alternative View," *Wadabagei: A Journal of the Caribbean and Its Diasporas* 13, no. 3 (2012): 74–94.

2. The young girl's belief that I was Bahamian also alerts us to how Bahamians—at least those from Nassau, New Providence—resemble Americans in appearance and dress.

3. Haitian Protestant churches in New Providence take on similar importance for Haitians living in New Providence, Bahamas.

4. Mass tourism in the Bahamas is characterized by the introduction of large hotel chains, large-scale gambling, and the cruise ship industry (Saunders 2000).

5. The Out Islands in the Bahamas are the least densely populated islands in the Bahamas such as Andros, Eleuthera, and Exuma.

6. Haiti became the poorest country in the Western Hemisphere under the Duvalier regime (1957–1986). For example, under Jean-Claude Duvalier's rule (1971–1986), the majority of Haitians slipped into poverty while Duvalier and the members of his inner circle grew fabulously rich. The percentage of the Haitian population living in extreme poverty rose from 48 percent in 1976 to 81 percent in 1985. Throughout this time, the Duvalier regime enjoyed US government support, including the American-chartered jet that picked up Duvalier from Haiti in 1986.

7. According to Tinker (2011, 105), "Operation Clean Up" was discontinued after less than a year because "the threat of conflict between Haiti and the Dominican Republic preoccupied Haitian officials and apparently prevented them from effective cooperation in the deportation process."

8. St. Jacques (2001, 60) notes the years of the three additional campaigns coincided with economic recessions and parliamentary election, periods when immigration was a contentious issue.

9. Johnson (1991, 125) locates the "Bahamas for the Bahamians" sentiment in the late 1920s when measures were adopted in the Bahamas to restrict the flow of immigrants.

10. Eloise, interview with the author, July 25, 2005.

11. I use the terms Bahamians of Haitian descent and Haitian-Bahamian interchangeably. Both terms refer to the children of Haitians born in the Bahamas. They are different from Haitians who were born and raised in Haiti and then migrated to the Bahamas. The Bahamian state does not make this distinction and refers to both groups as Haitian.

12. Those who obtain Bahamian passports are legally considered to be Bahamian. Whether they are socially considered to be Bahamian depends on the contexts they take part in.

13. At times Haitians and Bahamians of Haitian descent refer to the discrimination they have experienced in the Bahamas as racism although the overwhelming majority of Bahamians, Haitians, and Bahamians of Haitian descent are black (of African descent). I believe this sentiment stems from the general belief that there are innate,

fixed characteristics about Haitians that could destroy Bahamian social and political stability. Those beliefs are expressed in comments by the Bahamian populace about Haitians "takin' over" the Bahamas and crimes committed by Haitians.

14. In Bahamian English, speakers use the present tense to refer to the past tense.

15. Reginald, interview with the author, New Providence, Bahamas, September 12, 2005.

CHAPTER 3. PASTORS, CHURCHES, AND HAITIAN PROTESTANT TRANS-NATIONAL TIES

1. At the time of our interview Brother Frantz believed there was another Haitian evangelical church behind Victory Chapel Church of the Nazarene that had a small congregation. Interview with the author, New Providence, Bahamas, November 3, 2005.

2. This estimate is based on a list of Haitian pastors and their churches in New Providence given to me by Pastor Kevin Pierre in July 2012.

3. I chose to conduct my research in New Providence because this is where we find the majority of the population of the Bahamas (two-thirds of the overall Bahamian population). And New Providence is where we tend to find the majority of Haitians in the Bahamas.

4. Dr. Antoine St. Louis, interview with the author, New Providence, Bahamas, November 11, 2005.

5. Ibid.

6. I was originally awarded a Fulbright grant to continue my research about Protestantism in Haiti in 2004 but due to a coup d'état that removed then President Aristide from office, the Fulbright Program closed its office in the Haitian capital of Port-au-Prince and informed me that I would have to find another nation to conduct my research by March 2005 or I would have to return my Fulbright award in full.

7. To my knowledge, Fulbright no longer sponsors awards for research to the Bahamas.

8. Dr. Chérélus Exanté, interview with the author, New Providence, Bahamas, December 6, 2005.

9. Dr. Chérélus Exanté, interview with the author, New Providence, Bahamas, December 13, 2005.

10. Dr. Antoine St. Louis, interview with the author, New Providence, Bahamas, March 30, 2005.

11. At that time in 1988 there were less than ten Protestant Haitian churches in Nassau. In 2005 there were at least twenty.

12. Dr. Saint Louis received his doctorate after three and a half years of training in Nassau.

13. The dividing line here is not by age but by whether churchgoers are migrants or born in the Bahamas. In my observation, thirty-year-olds and older were regular attendees at *lajènes* meetings.

14. Pastor Kevin Pierre, interview with the author, New Providence, Bahamas, July 29, 2005.

15. Ibid.

16. Ibid.

17. While I attended the International Crusade in May 2005, I noted that at least seven churches were represented at the proceedings: the three churches in my study (Victory Chapel Church of the Nazarene, New Haitian Mission Baptist Church, International Tabernacle of Praise Ministries) and Jerusalem Baptist Church, Carmichael Evangelical Church, Calvary Haitian Baptist Church, Metropolitan Church of the Nazarene, and United Bethesda Baptist Church.

18. Earlier in our interview Dr. Védrine discussed his work among the Haitian diaspora in Boston:

> In terms of my missionary work in the Haitian diaspora, I am connected to two groups. One group is called Emmanuel Gospel Center where I serve as a ministry consultant to pastors in Boston and beyond and also a Baptist group in Chicago. Between my church and the group in Boston and Chicago, I have been in contact with Haitians over the past twenty years. I've also been in contact with a pastor in the Bahamas and Haiti as well.
>
> In Boston, because of our connection with Emmanuel Gospel Center, I have been bringing Haitian pastors together. The formal name of this group is the Fellowship of Haitian Evangelical Pastors of New England and I am the founder and have been the president of the organization for many years. When we meet we have pastor conferences, pastor retreats and a big gospel outreach.

19. Dr. Soliny Védrine, interview with the author, October 29, 2004.

20. Ibid.

21. The International Crusade is a prime example of how uneven effects occur when diasporas meet within a transnational social field. The sessions went overtime each night except when the Victory Chapel Church of the Nazarene *lajènes* was in charge. The fact that the crusade failed to end on time most of the time demonstrated a disconnect between those who were in charge of the crusade (which some viewed more as a revival than a crusade) and those who attended. Specifically, Haitians living in the Bahamas had to go to work early in the morning to work in construction or clean homes and resorts. Keeping them there at irregular hours of the night interrupted their sleeping patterns and supported a general indifference about the event. Although the crusade passed out provisions (toothpaste and food, for example) and clothes to the people of *Bwapen*, a Haitian settlement in New Providence, and provided free health clinics and consultations to the Haitian community, the sermons delivered throughout the week neither addressed the living conditions of Haitians in the Bahamas nor the hell Haitians in the Bahamas were catching. Many informants felt that there was too much talking by the foreign contingent and too many introductions and the foreign pastors were massaging their egos along with the pastors who had invited them. Some people in the community said that they would not attend future crusades for these reasons.

CHAPTER 4. HAITIAN PROTESTANT LUTURGY

1. See Mapuranga and Chitando (2006) for an example of how gospel music in Zimbabwe conveyed hope, healing, and regeneration to the people of Zimbabwe.

2. These include Protestant denominations (Baptist, Anglican, Pentecostal, and Methodist) and Roman Catholicism.

3. Ryrie Study Bible, New International Version. Chicago: Moody Press, 1994, 1591.

CHAPTER 5. "THE PEOPLE WHO HAVE NOT CONVERTED YET," PROTESTANT, AND CHRISTIAN

1. See the Preeclampsia website, http://www.preeclampsia.org/about-us.

2. Field notes from Victory Chapel Church of the Nazarene. December 11, 2005. New Providence, Bahamas.

3. This caricature of Haitian Catholics was created through formal and informal interviews with Haitian Protestants living in New Providence, Bahamas.

4. Biblical teachings, denominational doctrines, and indigenous and foreign evangelization that stressed a strict type of appearance and comportment also contributed to the development of Haitian Protestant religious culture.

5. Brother Jonas, interview with the author, New Providence, Bahamas, September 4, 2005.

6. Another thing that Brother Jonas did not like about church life in New Providence, was that services never seemed to start on time, nor end on time for that matter. In Haiti, church services always started and ended on time. To him Protestant churches in Haiti always followed this principle but his church in New Providence ignored it. Not only did his church in Nassau ignore the time but the congregants did as well. He also stated that the church he attended in Haiti used French more than Haitian Creole throughout church services. New Haitian Mission conducted church services primarily in Haitian Creole.

7. Brother Jonas, interview.

8. For an in-depth discussion of *plasaj* and conjugality in Haiti, see Lowenthal (1987).

9. Brother Jonas, interview.

10. Ryrie Study Bible, New International Version. Chicago: Moody Press, 1994, 1768.

11. Ibid., 1769.

12. Ibid., 1854.

13. Sister Maude, interview.

14. *Plasaj* is the union between a man and a woman recognized by public opinion, but not by law (Métraux 1959: 377). Specifically, in the region that most Haitians who migrate to the Bahamas come from, Haiti's Northwestern department, *plasaj* is a common practice between men and women.

15. Sister Maude, interview.

16. Ibid.

17. Brother Nicholas, interview with the author, October 9, 2005.

18. Ibid.

19. Ibid.

20. Ibid.

21. In my opinion Brother Nicholas's example does not constitute a Protestant "practicing" Vodou. A *Pwotestan* is not necessarily practicing Vodou when he or she consults a Vodou priest. To practice Vodou is to serve *lwa* (ancestral spirits) and feed them when it is required. What he describes is simply a consult where the possibility of ill will comes in the form of *maji* (sorcery), for example.

22. Brother Nicholas, interview.

23. In an interview with the author (Saint Peters, Missouri, June 13, 2004), Jean L. Paillan, the former head pastor of Truth and Grace Haitian Christian Church in Saint Peters, Missouri, described what it meant to him to be a Christian and its challenges in reference to Christianity: "The challenge is to have one being living his faith at every aspect in life: whether you are in business, politics, whether you are a minister, whether you are a teacher, wherever you go. You are a Christian and you carry with you principles that you will apply in every setting. Those principles are very clear, my friend. It comes down to your character: honesty, integrity, and transparence as a person. These are the things that Christ taught and these are the things that are missing not only in Haitian society but the world over."

24. I borrow from Butler's (2002) argument about Pentecostal Haitian identity and Haitian Nationalism.

25. *Konpa*, a popular Haitian music form that some Protestant denominations embrace and others reject, is performed at *bal* (dances) and nightclubs in Haiti and its diaspora. Haitian Protestants of different denominations listen to and perform evangelical versions of hymns and original compositions within the transnational social field discussed in this chapter.

26. See Glick Schiller and Fouron (2001).

CONCLUSION

1. According to the CIA World Factbook, https://www.cia.gov/library/publications/the-world-factbook/geos/bf.html, the Bahamas is 67.6 percent Protestant (Baptist 35.4 percent, Anglican 15.1 percent, Pentecostal 8.1 percent, Church of God 4.8 percent, Methodist 4.2 percent), 13.5 percent Roman Catholic, 15.2 percent other Christian, 2.9 percent none or unspecified, and 0.8 percent other (based on the 2000 census).

2. See the Church of God Prophecy website, http://www.cogop.org.

3. Brother Jean-Baptiste, interview with the author, New Providence, Bahamas. November 11, 2005.

REFERENCES

Alexander, M. Jacqui. 1997. "Erotic Autonomy as a Politics of Decolonization: An Anatomy of Feminist and State Practice in the Bahamas Tourist Economy." In *Feminist Genealogies, Colonial Legacies, Democratic Futures*, edited by M. Jacqui Alexander and Chandra Talpade Mohanty, 63–100 New York: Routledge.

Arthur, Charles, and Michael Dash, eds. 1999. *Libète: A Haiti Anthology*. Kingston, JM: Ian Randle Publishers.

Atkinson, Robert. 1998. *The Life Story Interview*. Thousand Oaks, CA: Sage Publications.

Austin-Broos, Diane. 1997. *Jamaican Genesis: Religion and the Politics of Moral Orders*. Chicago: The University of Chicago Press.

Bahaman Constitution. 1973. http://pdba.georgetown.edu/Constitutions/Bahamas/bah73.html. Accessed February 8, 2007.

Barrick, Michael. 2005. "Evangelical Leader to Seek Haitian Presidency: Chavannes Jeune Looking to Reverse 200 Years of Corruption and Poverty." *Lincoln Tribune*, August 6.

Barth, Frederick. 1969. Introduction. In *Ethnic Groups and Boundaries: The Social Organization of Culture Difference*, edited by Frederick Barth, 9–38. Boston, MA: Little, Brown and Company.

Basch, Linda, Nina Glick Schiller, and Cristina Szanton Blanc. 1994. *Nations Unbound: Transnational Projects, Postcolonial Predicaments, and Deterritorialized Nation-States*. Langhorne: Gordon and Breach.

Berg, Charles Ramírez. 1997. "Stereotyping in Films in General and of the Hispanic in Particular." In *Latin Looks: Images of Latinas and Latinos in the American Media*, 104–120. Boulder, CO: Westview Press.

Bernard, H. Russell. 2002. *Research Methods in Anthropology: Qualitative and Quantitative Approaches*. 3rd ed. Walnut Creek, CA: AltaMira Press.

Bethel, Nicolette. 2000. "Navigations: National Identity and the Archipelago." In *Yinna. Volume I. Journal of the Bahamas Association for Cultural Studies (BACUS)*, 21–38. Nassau: Guanima Press Ltd.

Bourdieu, Pierre. 1999. *Language and Symbolic Power*. Cambridge, MA: Harvard University Press.

Brodwin, Paul. 2003a. "Marginality and Subjectivity in the Haitian Diaspora." *Anthropological Quarterly* 76, no. 3: 383–410.

———. 2003b. "Pentecostalism in Translation: Religion and the Production of Community in the Haitian Diaspora." *American Ethnologist* 30, no 1: 85–101.

Brown, Karen McCarthy. 1991. *Mama Lola: A Vodou Priestess in Brooklyn.* Berkeley: University of California Press.

Brusco, Elizabeth. 1995. *The Reformation of Machismo: Evangelical Conversion and Gender in Colombia.* Austin: University of Texas Press.

Butler, Melvin. 2002. "'Nou Kwe nan Sentespri'/'We Believe in the Holy Spirit': Music, Ecstasy and Identity in Haitian Pentecostal Worship." *Black Music Research Journal* 22, no. 1: 85–125

Cannell, Fenella. 2006. *The Anthropology of Christianity*, edited by Fenella Cannell. Durham, NC: Duke University Press.

Chants D'espérance, Quarante deuxième édition. 1995. Port-au-Prince, HT: Imprimerie Henri Deschamps.

Chestnut, Andrew. 2003. *Competitive Spirits: Latin America's New Religious Economy.* New York: Oxford University Press.

College of the Bahamas. 2005. "Haitian Migrants in the Bahamas: A Report for the International Organization for Migration." http://iom.int/jahia/webdav/site/myjahiasite/shared/shared/mainsite/published_docs/books/Haitian_Migrants_Report.pdf.

Collinwood, Dean W., and Steve Dodge. 1989. *Modern Bahamian Society.* Parkersburg, IA: Caribbean Books.

Comaroff, Jean, and John Comaroff. 1991. *Of Revelation and Revolution: Christianity, Colonialism, and Consciousness in South Africa.* Chicago: University of Chicago Press.

Conway, Frederick. 1978. "Pentecostalism in the Context of Haitian Religion and Health Practice." PhD diss., Department of Anthropology, American University, Washington, DC.

Corten, André. 2001. *Misère, religion et politique en Haïti : Diabolisation et mal politique.* Montréal: Karthala.

Craton, Michael. 1995. "The Bahamian Self and the Haitian Other: The Migration of Haitians to and through the Bahamas, 1950–2000." *Immigrants and Minorities* 3: 265–288.

Craton, Michael, and Gail Saunders. 1992. *Islanders in the Stream: A History of the Bahamian People.* Vol. 1, *From Aboriginal Times to the End of Slavery.* Athens: University of Georgia Press.

———. 1998. *Islanders in the Stream: A History of the Bahamian People.* Vol. 2, *From the Ending of Slavery to the Twenty-First Century.* Athens: University of Georgia Press.

Desmangles, Leslie. 1992. *The Faces of the Gods: Vodou and Roman Catholicism in Haiti.* Chapel Hill: University of North Carolina Press.

Dupuy, Alex. 1989. *Haiti in the World Economy: Class, Race and Underdevelopment since 1700.* Boulder, CO: Westview Press.

Ebaugh, Helen Rose, and Janet Saltzman Chafetz, eds. 2002. *Religion Across Borders: Transnational Immigrant Networks.* Walnut Creek, CA: AltaMira Press.

Farmer, Paul. 1994. *The Uses of Haiti*. Monroe, ME: Common Courage Press.

Fick, Carolyn. 1990. *The Making of Haiti: The Saint-Domingue Revolution from Below*. Knoxville: University of Tennessee Press.

Fielding, William, Virginia Balance, Carol Scriven, Thaddeus McDonald, and Pandora Johnson. 2008. "The Stigma of Being 'Haitian' in the Bahamas." *College of the Bahamas Research Journal* 14: 38–50.

Gates, Henry Louis Jr. 2010. "The Curse on Haiti." *The Root*. January 25. http://www.theroot.com/articles/history/2010/01/pat_robertson_was_wrong_the_curse_on_haiti_came_from_thomas_jefferson.html.

Geertz, Clifford. 1973. "Deep Play: Notes on the Balinese Cockfight." In *The Interpretation of Cultures*, 412–453. New York, NY: Basic Books.

Geggus, David. 1982. *Slavery, War and Revolution: The British Occupation of Saint-Domingue, 1793–1798*. New York: Oxford University Press.

Germain, Felix. 2011. "The Earthquake, The Missionaries, and the Future of Vodou." *Journal of Black Studies* 42, no. 2: 247–263.

Glick Schiller, Nina, and Georges Fouron. 2001. *Georges Woke Up Laughing: Long-Distance Nationalism and the Search for Home*. Durham, NC: Duke University Press.

Guadeloupe, Francio. 2009. *Chanting Down the New Jerusalem: Calypso, Christianity, and Capitalism in the Caribbean*. Berkeley: University of California Press.

Harding, Susan. 1987. "Convicted by the Holy Ghost: The Rhetoric of Fundamental Baptist Conversion." *American Ethnologist* 14, no. 1: 167–181.

———. 1991. "Representing Fundamentalism: The Problem of the Repugnant Cultural Other." *Social Research* 58, no. 2: 373–393.

———. 2000. *The Book of Jerry Falwell: Fundamentalist Language and Politics*. Princeton, NJ: Princeton University Press.

Hefner, Robert W. 1993. "World Building and the Rationality of Conversion." In *Conversion to Christianity: Historical and Anthropological Perspectives on a Great Transformation*, edited by Robert Hefner, 3–44. Berkeley: University of California Press.

Heneise, Ivah. 1999. *Pioneers of Light: Stories of the Baptist Witness in Haiti: 1823–1998*. Penney Farms, FL: International Christian Education Fund.

Holm, John A., and Alison Shilling. 1982. *Dictionary of Bahamian English*. Cold Spring, NY: Lexik House Publishers.

Houtart, François, and Anselme Rémy. 1997. *Les référents culturels à Port-au-Prince*. Port-au-Prince: CRESFED.

Howell, Brian. 2007. "The repugnant cultural other speaks back: Christian identity as ethnographic 'standpoint.'" *Anthropological Theory* 7: 371–391.

Hurbon, Laënnec. 2001. "Pentecostalism and Transnationalisation in the Caribbean." In *Between Babel and Pentecost: Transnational Pentecostalism in Africa and Latin America*, edited by André Corten and Ruth Marshall-Fratani, 124–141. Bloomington: Indiana University Press.

James, C. L. R. 1963. *The Black Jacobins: Toussaint Louverture and the San Domingo Revolution*. New York: Random House.

Jeanty, Edner A. 1993. *Diksyonè Kreyòl: Dictionary Angle-Kreyòl, Kreyòl-Angle*. Port-au-Prince: La Presse Evangelique.

Johnson, Howard. 1991. *The Bahamas in Slavery and Freedom*. Kingston, JM: Ian Randle Publishers Ltd.

———. 2000. "National Identity and Bahamian Culture." In *Yinna. Volume I. Journal of the Bahamas Association for Cultural Studies (BACUS)*, 13–20. Nassau: Guanima Press Ltd.

Keane, Webb. *Christian Moderns: Freedom and Fetish in the Mission Encounter*. Berkeley: University of California Press, 2007.

Keyes, Charles F. 2002. "Weber and Anthropology." *Annual Review of Anthropology* 31: 233–255.

Kidder, Tracy. 2003. *Mountains Beyond Mountains*. New York: Random House.

Lamont, Michèle. 1992. *Money, Morals and Manners: The Culture of the French and American Upper-Middle Class*. Chicago: University of Chicago Press.

Lamont, Michèle, and Virag Molnar. 2002. "The Study of Boundaries in the Social Sciences." *Annual Review of Sociology* 28: 167–95.

Lewis, Oscar. 1968. "The Culture of Poverty." In *On Understanding Poverty: Perspectives from the Social Sciences*. New York: Basic Books.

Louis, Jr., Bertin M. 2003. "To Cut or Not to Cut: A Hair-Raising Anthropological Fieldwork Dilemma in Port-au-Prince, Haiti." In *Anthropology News*. National Association of Student Anthropologists (NASA) Column. November.

———. 2010. "Haiti's pact with the devil? (Some Haitians believe this too)." *The Immanent Frame Blog*. http://blogs.ssrc.org/tif/2010/02/18/haitis-pact-with-the-devil-some-haitians-believe-this-too/.

———. 2011. "Haitian Protestant Views of *Vodou* and the Importance of *Karacktè* (Character) within a Transnational Social Field." *Journal of Haitian Studies* 17, no. 1 (Spring): 211–227.

———. 2012a. "The Haitian Diaspora of the Bahamas: An Alternative View." *Wadabagei: A Journal of the Caribbean and Its Diasporas* 13, no. 3: 74–94.

———. 2012b. "*Touloutoutou* and *Tet Mare* Churches: Language, Class and Protestantism in the Haitian Diaspora of the Bahamas." *Studies in Religion/Sciences Religieuses* 41, no. 2: 216–230.

Lowenthal, Ira. 1987. "'Marriage Is 20, Children Are 21:' The Cultural Construction of Conjugality and the Family in Rural Haiti." PhD diss., Department of Anthropology, The Johns Hopkins University, Baltimore, MD.

Maynard, Kent. 1993. "Protestant Theories and Anthropological Knowledge: Convergent Models in the Ecuadorian Sierra." *Cultural Anthropology* 8, no. 2: 246–267.

Mapuranga, Tapiwa, and Ezra Chitando. 2006. "Songs of Healing and Regeneration: Pentecostal Gospel Music in Zimbabwe." *Religion and Theology* 13, no. 1: 72–89.

Matory, J. Lorand. 2005. *Black Atlantic Religion: Tradition, Transnationalism and Matriarchy in the Afro-Brazilian Candomblé*. Princeton, NJ: Princeton University Press.

Marshall, Dawn. 1979. *"The Haitian Problem": Illegal Migration to the Bahamas*. University of the West Indies. Kingston, JM: Institute of Social and Economic Research.

McAlister, Elizabeth. 1998. "The Madonna of 115th Street Revisited: Vodou and Haitian Catholicism in the Age of Transnationalism." In *Gatherings in Diaspora: Religious Communities and the New Immigration*, edited by R. Stephen Warner and Judith G. Wittner, 123–160. Philadelphia, PA: Temple University Press, 1998.

———. 2006. "Spiritual Warfare and the Evangelical Re-writing Of History in Haiti." Paper prepared for the Anthropology and History Workshop, University of Michigan, September 15.

———. 2012. "From Slave Revolt to a Blood Pact with Satan: The Evangelical Rewriting of Haitian History." *Studies in Religion/Sciences Religieuses*. June 12. Published online before print on April 25, doi: 10.1177/0008429812441310.

Métraux, Alfred. 1959. *Voodoo in Haiti*. New York: Oxford University Press.

Miller, Lisa. 2010. "Miller: Haiti and the Theology of Suffering." Newsweek. January 14. http://www.newsweek.com/miller-haiti-and-theology-suffering-71231.

Mooney, Margarita. 2009. *Faith Makes Us Live: Surviving and Thriving in the Haitian Diaspora*. Berkeley: University of California Press.

Nassau Guardian. 2005. "Illegals must go says Miller." February 10.

Ng, Alicia. 2006. "Evangelism Spreads throughout Haitian Communities. *New American Media*. February 28. http://news.newamericamedia.org/news/view_article. html?article_id=764eab64c5229a37356b9faf052bc638.

Novick, Peter. 1999. *The Holocaust in American Life*. Boston, MA: Houghton Mifflin.

Portes, Alejandro, Luis Guarnizo, and Patricia Landolt. 1999. "Introduction: Pitfalls and Promise of an Emergent Research Field." *Ethnic and Racial Studies* 22, no. 2: 217–238.

Rey, Terry, and Alex Stepick. 2010. "Visual Culture and Visual Piety in Little Haiti: The Sea, the Tree, and the Refugee." In *Art in the Lives of Immigrant Communities in the U.S.*, edited by Paul DiMaggio and Patricia Fernández-Kelly, 229–248. New Brunswick, NJ: Rutgers University Press.

Richman, Karen. 2005a. *Migration and Vodou*. Gainesville: University of Florida Press.

———. 2005b. "The Protestant Ethic and the Dis-Spirit of Vodou." In *Immigrant Faiths: Transforming Religious Life in America*, edited by Karen I. Leonard, 165–185. Walnut Creek, CA: AltaMira Press.

———. 2012. "Religion at the Epicenter: Agency and Affiliation in Léogâne after the Earthquake." *Studies in Religion/Sciences Religieuses*. June 12. Published online before print on April 25, doi:10.1177/0008429812441314.

Robbins, Joel. 2004a. *Becoming Sinners: Christianity and Moral Torment in a Papua New Guinea Society*. Berkeley: University of California Press.

———. 2004b. "The Globalization of Pentecostal and Charismatic Christianity." *Annual Review of Anthropology* 33: 117–43.

Romain, Charles P. 1986. *Le protestantisme dans la société haïtienne: Contribution à l'étude sociologique d'une religion (Prèmiere Edition)*. Port-au-Prince: Imprimerie Henri Deschamps.

———. 2004. *Le protestantisme dans la société haïtienne: Contribution à l'étude sociologique d'une religion (Deuxième Edition)*. Coconut Creek, FL: Educa Vision.

Rouse, Roger. 1991. "Mexican Migration and the Social Space of Postmodernism." *Diaspora* 1, no. 1: 8–23.

Ryrie Study Bible. 1994. Exp. ed., New International Version. Chicago: Moody Press, 1994.

Saint Louis, Judy Carol. 1999. "An Investigation of the Plights of and Deprivations Faced within the Bahamian Society by Children Born in the Bahamas to Haitian Parents." Unpublished manuscript.

Saunders, Gail. 2000. "The Impact of Tourism on Bahamian Culture: A Historical Perspective." In *Yinna: Journal of the Bahamas Association for Cultural Studies (BACUS)*. Vol. 1, 72–87. Nassau: Guanima Press Ltd.

Schieffelin, Bambi, and Rachelle Charlier Doucet. 1994. The "Real" Haitian Creole: Ideology, Metalinguistics and Orthographic Choice. *American Ethnologist* 21, no. 1: 176–200.

Stoll, David. 1990. *Is Latin America Turning Protestant? The Politics of Evangelical Growth*. Berkeley: University of California Press.

Strachan, Ian. 2002. *Paradise and Plantation: Tourism and Culture in the Anglophone Caribbean*. Charlottesville: University of Virginia Press.

St. Jacques, Ermitte. 2001. "'Today Haitians, Tomorrow Bahamians': Reassessing the Integration of Haitian Immigrants in the Bahamas." MA thesis, University of Florida, Gainesville.

Stromberg, Peter. 1993. *Language and Self-Transformation: A Study of the Christian Conversion Narrative*. Cambridge, Melbourne, and New York: Cambridge University Press.

Tinker, Keith. 2011. *The Migration of Peoples from the Caribbean to the Bahamas*. Gainesville: University Press of Florida.

Treco, Ria. 2002. "The Haitian Diaspora in the Bahamas." Unpublished manuscript, Department of International Relations, Florida International University.

Tsuda, Takeyuki. 2003. *Strangers in the Ethnic Homeland: Japanese Brazilian Return Migration in Transnational Perspective*. New York: Columbia University Press.

Vilsaint, Féquière. 1991. *Diksyonè Kreyòl Angle*. Temple Terrace, FL: Educa Vision.

Waterston, Alisse. 2006. "Are Latinos Becoming 'White' Folk? And What That Still Says about Race in America." *Transforming Anthropology* 14, no. 2: 133–150.

Weber, Max. [1930] 1995. *The Protestant Ethic and the Spirit of Capitalism*. New York: Routledge.

Woodson, Drexel G., and Mamadou A. Baro. 1996. *A Baseline Study of Livelihood Security in the Southern Peninsula of Haiti*. Tucson: Bureau of Applied Research in Anthropology, University of Arizona.

———. 1997. *A Baseline Study of Livelihood Security in the Department of the Artibonite, Center, North, Northeast, and West, Republic of Haiti*. Tucson: Bureau of Applied Research in Anthropology, University of Arizona.

Yale Human Rights Delegation Report. 1994. Human Rights Delegation Report on Haitians in the Bahamas (cited February 8, 2007). http://www.yale.edu/lawweb/avalon/diana/haiti/haitibahama.htm.

INDEX

ABOUT THE AUTHOR

Bertin M. Louis, Jr., is Assistant Professor of Anthropology and Afri-
cana Studies, a core faculty member of the Disasters, Displacement, and
Human Rights program of the Department of Anthropology, affiliated
faculty in American Studies, and a Faculty Fellow of the Center for the
Study of Social Justice, Global Studies, and Latin American and Caribbean Studies at the University of Tennessee, Knoxville.